D1550572

OWN IT
AND
KEEP IT

For Jeff Butler
With Best Wishes —

Ted Hughes
6/7/00

Own It
and
Keep It

Revised Edition

Theodore E. Hughes
and
David Klein

AN INFOBASE HOLDINGS COMPANY

Own It and Keep It

Facts On File, Inc.
460 Park Avenue South
New York NY 10016

Library of Congress Cataloging-in-Publication Data

Hughes, Theodore E.
Own it and keep it / Theodore E. Hughes and David Klein.
p. cm.
Includes index.
Rev. Ed. of: Ownership. 1984.
ISBN 0-8160-3279-3 (acid-free paper)
1. Estate planning—United States—Popular works. 2. Tax planning—United States—Popular works. 3. Property—United States—Popular works. I. Klein, David. 1919-   . II. Hughes, Theodore E. Ownership. III. Title.
KF750.Z9H84   1995
346.7305′2—dc20
[347.30652]   94-42399

Facts On File books are available at special discounts when purchased in bulk quantities for businesses, associations, institutions or sales promotions. Please call our Special Sales Department in New York at 212/683-2244 or 800/322-8755.

Jacket design by Dorothy Wachtenheim

Printed in the United States of America

MP TT 10 9 8 7 6 5 4 3 2 1

This book is printed on acid-free paper.

FOR
Elizabeth and Marymae
our respective tenants by the entirety

CONTENTS

FIGURES

TABLES

A NOTE TO THE READER

The aim of this book is to help you manage whatever assets you have so that you retain maximum control over them, both during your lifetime and after your death, so that they are not needlessly eroded by income taxes during your lifetime, and so that, on your death, they pass swiftly and undepleted into the hands of your chosen beneficiaries with minimum exposure to probate administration, court costs, executors' fees, lawyers' and accountants' fees, and death taxes. All these ends can be accomplished if you choose the right form of ownership for the various assets you own or expect to own.

Most books of this kind, because they are written for the rich—or, rather, for their legal and tax advisors—tend to emphasize tax shelters and other tactics that are simply not practical for most people. This book is addressed to people of moderate means, for whom the careful husbanding of assets is even more important.

Every option described in this book is "safe" in two respects: None requires that you put your assets at risk or beyond your control, and each has been unambiguously approved by the Internal Revenue Service. Moreover, some of the most practical tactics we propose—custodial accounts, for example, or joint tenancies, or bank account trusts—can be set up simply and quickly, without the help of a lawyer and usually at no cost.

Not every ownership alternative can be presented responsibly in do-it-yourself terms. Although both living trusts and closely held corporations prove exceedingly useful for some middle-income families, it is hazardous to try to establish either one without the help of an experienced lawyer, because the standard prefabricated do-it-yourself forms cannot accurately reflect your individual circumstances or the idiosyncrasies of your state's laws.

Even if you suspect that petty differences among state laws exist to ensure full employment for the legal and accounting professions, you will probably be better off paying a one-time professional fee than suffering the losses and delays that can result if you choose an unsuitable ownership option or if your homemade trust document or corporate charter is disqualified because it is defective in some trivial but legally significant way.

As you scan the table of contents or skim through the text, we would urge you not to skip certain chapters simply because such phrases as "successor trustee" or "corporate officer" strike you as too rich for your blood. Although trusts and corporations have been traditionally favored by the very rich, the advantages they offer are equally available to you—often at surprisingly low cost.

OWN IT
AND
KEEP IT

C H A P T E R 1

WHAT OWNERSHIP MEANS

Owning something—a bank account, an automobile, a house—is so commonplace that most of us don't give it much thought. Ever since the age of two or three, when we first experienced the delightful difference between "It's mine!" and "It's my sister's," we've tended to assume that "It's mine" is a convenient abbreviation of "It's all mine, and I can do whatever I please with it."

But we really know better, of course. Our rights of ownership of material goods are by no means absolute. Both the amount of property we can accumulate and the uses we can make of it are restricted by society as it attempts to strike a balance between the haves and the have-nots—between the interests of the owners of private property and the welfare of other people and of society as a whole.

The restraints on ownership rights for the sake of social peace and harmony are not, of course, an American invention. They appear, at least to some extent, in every society. In tribal societies that lived by fishing and hunting, the catch or the game was shared by everyone, regardless of who owned the canoe or made the kill. In our own much more complex society, we are required both during our lives and after death to share our property with our spouses and minor children, to pay our debts, and to give the government part of our assets to finance public services and to support those who cannot support themselves.

1

In primitive societies, this balance between private gain and public welfare was enforced by custom, and by shaming or shunning those who jeopardized it. In modern societies, government agencies—the courts, the tax authorities, and the pension and welfare agencies—maintain the balance, and they enforce it through taxes, fees, fines, and other legal penalties.

Our own society, from its very beginnings, has generally favored the accumulation of private property rather than the good of the community as a whole. Indeed, the Declaration of Independence in one of its earlier drafts specified the "inalienable rights" as "life, liberty, and *property*," rather than "the pursuit of happiness." And today, to a greater degree than in most other modern societies, Americans are encouraged, by law, by custom, and by their value system, to accumulate as much property as they possibly can. Most of us tend to evaluate other people on the basis of the material possessions they have accumulated or inherited. More important, each individual's "life chances"—that is, the level of education he is likely to complete, the kind of career he is likely to pursue, his general level of health, and his life expectancy—depend directly on his net worth.

Rights and Responsibilities of Ownership

The American attitude toward private ownership is highly permissive, but it is not totally unrestrained. Our laws prohibit us from owning certain kinds of things—narcotics and machine guns, for example—that are regarded as harmful to ourselves or to the community as a whole, and we are not allowed to use what we do own in ways that may harm others. Our possessions are taxed, not only to pay for public services and social welfare but also to discourage excessive accumulation and to redistribute our wealth for the general social good. Various laws prevent our accumulating property for ourselves at the expense of those to whom we have social obligations: our families, our creditors, our employees, and the government.

In addition, the government influences our choices of *what* to own by using the tax system to reward us for owning things that are regarded, rightly or wrongly, as beneficial for society as a whole. Thus, because home ownership is regarded as good, homeowners are permitted to deduct property taxes and mortgage interest from their taxable income, a privilege not directly available to renters. Similarly, because the funding of public works is seen as socially desirable, the yields from certain kinds of municipal and state bonds are tax exempt.

You can see the interplay between private and public interest by reviewing each of the basic rights that you have with respect to property you own and the restrictions and obligations that limit these rights.

You have the right to enjoy its use, but you may not use it in any way that infringes upon the comfort or safety of other people. If you own a summer cottage, you can use it in any way you like—but not in ways that violate the zoning ordinances or the health code or that constitute a public nuisance. Moreover, you may be responsible for any injury in which your property is involved—for the death of a child who drowns in your swimming pool, even if he was trespassing at the time, or for the crippling of a pedestrian by your automobile, whether or not you were the driver.

You have the right to any income the property generates: dividends from stock, rents from real estate, royalties from mineral leases, publishing contracts, or patents. But you must pay any taxes due on this income.

You have the right to lease, mortgage, or sell it, or to give it away during your lifetime, but this right, too, is neither absolute nor unqualified. You must, for example, be an adult and mentally competent. If you are married, your spouse may have to consent to the transaction. And, of course, the transaction may be taxable.

You have the right to any insurance proceeds resulting from damage to or destruction of your property. Similarly, you have the right to any proceeds that result from condemnation under the law of eminent domain, but any liens or mortgages on the property must be satisfied first.

On your death, you have the right to specify its disposition. You may give it to whomever you choose, but you may not disinherit certain of your survivors or leave unpaid either your lawful debts or any state or federal taxes assessed against your estate. Often the disposition of your assets involves administration of your estate by the probate court—a sometimes long and usually an expensive procedure.

All of these property rights are subject to the claims of certain other people. Your spouse and minor children, for example, are legally entitled to support both during your lifetime and after your death, and they can make claims against your property or your estate if support is not forthcoming. Your creditors can attach your property if you fail to pay their claims. Your property can be attached also by government authorities at any level if you are delinquent in paying your taxes. In addition, ownership of property can disqualify you from certain public benefits – such as Medicaid – that involve a means test.

Maximizing the Benefits, Minimizing the Costs

The rational approach to ownership of property is to maximize its advantages – that is, to retain full control over your property and to manage it so as to increase its value, its yield, or both – while reducing to a minimum its exposure to taxes and its vulnerability to creditors, disaffected relatives, and others who might have claims on it, either before or after your death. There are several ways of doing this, but they need to be evaluated thoughtfully, because each involves certain costs: a loss of partial or full control of the property, a reduction in its potential to produce income, or its erosion by taxation.

Although there are some investments that enable you to show a tax-deductible loss, most of them involve unacceptable risk and are usable only by the very rich. One possibility, however, that is reasonably safe and available at most income levels is an investment in municipal bonds, the income from which is exempt from federal tax. (In many states, the income from municipal bonds issued within the state is also exempt from state income tax.)

You can determine whether a tax-free bond is better for you than a taxable investment by using a simple formula:

Interest rate of the bond ÷ (1 – your tax bracket)

and then comparing the result with the interest rate on a taxable investment. Thus, if you are in the 28% bracket and you are offered a tax-free bond that pays 6%, the formula 6 ÷ .72 would require a taxable investment yield of at least 8.33%. Municipal bonds can be bought through a broker or through a wide variety of mutual funds.

A second approach – more practical, more flexible, and available to people at all income levels – involves the way in which the property is held, because the vulnerability of any property to taxing authorities, to creditors, or to probate court administration is entirely dependent on *who owns it*.

To cite a simple example, if you are the sole owner of 100 shares of stock, the shares are subject to the claims of your creditors, and they will be subject to probate court administration and possibly to death taxes before they can be passed on to your beneficiaries. If, instead, you register them in joint tenancy with your child (see Chap. 3), they generally cannot be attached by your creditors and, on your death, their ownership passes automatically to your child, free of probate administration and, in some states, state inheritance taxes.

Similarly, if you are accumulating a nest egg for a child's college education, you are responsible for taxes on any income the funds produce until they are actually spent. If, on the other hand, you place the money into a custodial account under the Uniform Gifts to Minors Act (in some states called the Uniform Transfers to Minors Act) or into a trust for minors (see Chap. 4), the tax liability passes to your child, who is almost certain to be in a lower tax bracket than you.

If you own certain types of common stock, whether as sole owner or jointly with your spouse, you are personally responsible for paying income tax on 100 percent of the dividends. If, however, you can form a corporation and use that same stock as part of its working capital (see Chap. 5), the corporation can invest in high-yield stocks of domestic corporations because it is entitled to the 70% dividend exclusion.

If you are concerned about what will happen to your property after you die—perhaps because your spouse has no financial or management experience, or because you have a disabled child who may need lifetime care—you may want to consider putting part or all of your assets into some form of trust, a far wiser arrangement than transferring them by will. If you choose a revocable trust (see Chap. 4), you have full use of the assets as long as you live but you remain liable for income taxes. An irrevocable trust, on the other hand, may relieve you of the tax burden but does not permit you to use the assets or change your mind as to its later disposition.

Of course, not all of these strategies are cost-free. To begin with, they may involve some loss of control. Joint ownership with a spouse or child, for example, requires sharing control with the joint owner— a risky arrangement if your family situation becomes unstable. And some forms of ownership are irrevocable. If you transfer money into a custodial account for your child's education, for example, you cannot change your mind and recall the gift; your child automatically gets possession of the money at age 18, 19, or 21 (depending on state laws), regardless of his educational plans or ambitions or his ability to manage money.

But most forms of ownership are not all-or-nothing arrangements. Almost all of them can be started on a small scale, and usually several can be utilized to give you the best possible results. The basic purpose of this book is to identify the ownership options and show you how to benefit from each of the several forms in which you can own what you possess now and what you anticipate acquiring in later years.

CHAPTER 2

OWNING IT ALL BY YOURSELF

If you were to make an inventory of everything you own—from your handkerchiefs and your pocket calculator to your automobile, your home, and your securities—you would realize that the overwhelming majority of these assets belong to you alone and that you may have no documents proving that you own them. Although you may hold on to the bill of sale for your clock radio or your toaster until the warranty expires, most of what you own you simply regard as "mine," taking its ownership for granted and giving it no thought.

But because some of the items in your inventory—your home, your car, your securities portfolio, your bank accounts—have both high value and long life expectancy, their ownership is almost invariably documented. Your signature card at the bank, the certificate of title for your car, the deed to your house, the bill of sale for your 18th-century clock—are records that specify the ownership of the property they describe. If these documents carry your name alone, you are, of course, the sole owner. And because you are also the sole owner of hundreds of short-lived, disposable, and undocumented possessions, it is all too easy for you to take for granted that sole ownership is the best way to own everything.

Sole ownership is, indeed, the best way to own *some* of your possessions. But for many people in many situations, it is less than ideal. As you read the following discussion of the pros and cons of sole ownership, you may well find that some of the alternatives described in later chapters offer you distinct advantages, at least for some of the many things you own.

CONTROL AND MANAGEMENT

If you own something entirely by yourself, you can exercise almost complete control over it. Subject to the limitations mentioned in the preceding chapter, you can sell it, lease it, mortgage it, give it away, destroy it, or do almost anything you like with it during your lifetime, and you can decide who should inherit it after you die.

Given the many uncertainties of life today—the high divorce rate, the increasing number of midlife career shifts, the unpredictability of the economy, and the general weakening of family bonds—a high degree of control over what you own may have a good deal of value. If, for example, you are uncertain about the stability of your own marriage or the marriage of one of your children, if you have doubts about a child's educational or employment future, or if you foresee the possibility of someday starting a business venture that will require a substantial investment, then having your assets entirely under your own control can do wonders for your feelings of security, autonomy, freedom, and flexibility.

But this advantage comes at a price that you need to consider rather carefully. To begin with, sole ownership provides you with no protection against your own impulsive behavior. Whether a decision facing you involves a speculative investment, the disinheritance of a child, or a dramatic shift in your occupational career, the presence of a joint owner whose consent to your decision is necessary can serve as a buffer and can prevent you from acting precipitately or thoughtlessly.

Similarly, if the intelligent management of some of your assets— real estate, for example, or Treasury bills—requires more experience than you have or more attention than you can afford, a joint owner (see Chap. 3) or a trustee (see Chap. 4) may give your assets closer attention and better management than you yourself could.

A further shortcoming of sole ownership stems from the fact that as sole owner, you are the only person who can monitor and manage your assets; and that every once in a while some unanticipated action may have to be taken promptly in order to protect or increase them.

Such an event may strike you as improbable, but it occurs more frequently than many people believe, and it can have serious consequences.

Suppose, for example, that someone unexpectedly makes you an attractive offer for your summer cottage or tenders an offer for some stock you own. Or suppose that a sharp fluctuation in the stock market makes it profitable for you to buy or sell some of your securities immediately. If at that moment you are unavailable— because you are traveling abroad or, perhaps, because you are hospitalized—you may suffer substantial losses simply because you were not able to make the decision and do what needed to be done.

Worse yet, an accident or an illness may at any time leave you temporarily or permanently incompetent to make any decisions at all with respect to your property. If this happens, a guardian— sometimes called a conservator—will have to be nominated (and approved and supervised by the local probate court) to manage your affairs. But there are several legal constraints on what a guardian may do with your property. In some situations, your guardian may not, for example, sell any of your real estate without specific permission from the court. He may not make gifts on your behalf, even though you intended that such gifts be made. He may not make a will on your behalf or revoke or amend an existing one. His discretion to pay your bills and make other disbursements for you is severely limited. And he must file with the probate court a detailed annual accounting of your financial affairs, which will probably become a public record. Moreover, your guardian, however well-intentioned, may not have the experience needed to manage some kinds of property wisely.

One way to circumvent the limitations and costs inherent in a guardianship is to grant to one or more persons a *power of attorney*, which is done by signing and delivering a document giving them the authority to act on your behalf in specified circumstances. Spouses often give each other powers of attorney so that each can deal with the other's property should the need arise.

Powers of attorney are extremely flexible, and they can be written so as to suit your personal needs and financial situation quite precisely. Your power of attorney can, if you like, provide your "attorney in fact" (who need not be a lawyer but may be any adult you choose) with unlimited powers to do virtually anything on your behalf, or you may limit it to:

a specified period of time—for example, for the two months next summer during which you will be traveling in Asia; or for next week, when you will be in the hospital for surgery;

a specified purpose—for example, for selling your house; or for buying and selling securities in your brokerage account; or for making deposits in your bank account and writing checks against it;

a specified circumstance—for example, in the event of your temporary or permanent disability.

Historically, a power of attorney was automatically revoked if its grantor became mentally incompetent. Today, however, most states authorize the use of a "durable" power of attorney document, one that survives the grantor's mental incompetency if he or she expressly states this preference in the document. Your local probate court clerk can tell you whether your state recognizes the durable version. In all states, however, a power of attorney is automatically revoked upon death; hence, your designated "agent" can do nothing to manage or transfer any of the assets you leave behind.

Simple forms for granting a general power of attorney are available from office-supply stores, and special-purpose forms are usually available from banks and brokerage firms. The form shown in Figure 1, which is both comprehensive and "durable," may be useful if you plan to grant broad powers to one person. Once you have signed it, simply give it to the person you name as your agent so that he or she can present it when transacting business on your behalf.

There are alternative ways of handling some of your affairs when you are ill or out of town. Many banks, for a nominal fee, will pay your recurring bills and other obligations—utility and tax bills, for example, credit-card accounts, or mortgage payments. Most corporations, money market funds, and brokerage firms will, on your instruction, deposit your dividend and interest checks directly into your bank account. And most full-service stockbrokers are willing to convert your regular account to a discretionary account, which in effect gives your account executive a power of attorney for buying and selling securities on your behalf.

These are rather useful devices, but you may want to consider an alternative form of ownership for those assets that require constant vigilance and, occasionally, prompt action. If your bank account is registered in joint ownership with another person, either of the co-owners can manage it single-handedly, regardless of the whereabouts or current competence of the joint owner. If your securities are registered in the name of the trustee of a trust, the trustee can buy or

Figure 1
DURABLE POWER OF ATTORNEY

I, _____ , a resident of _____
County, Michigan, give this power of attorney, subject to the following
terms and conditions, and revoke all powers of attorney that I may
have given previously to the extent that they grant authority over my
property or financial affairs.

1. *Effective Date.* This power of attorney is effective upon execution.
   This power of attorney shall continue in effect until revoked by my
   written revocation or by my death.

2. *Agent.* I appoint _____ , my agent with
   respect to property and financial matters. If [he/she] is unable or
   unwilling to serve for whatever reason, I appoint _____ ,
   as successor with all of the powers given my original agent.

   A person may rely upon any act done by my substitute agent
   and shall not be required to ask whether my original agent is in
   fact unable or unwilling to serve.

3. *Powers of Agent.* I grant to my agent full power and authority to
   deal with my property and financial matters as fully as I could do
   personally. All powers shall be exercised in a fiduciary capacity in
   my best interests and for my welfare.

   This power of attorney includes, but is not limited to, the
   following specific powers:

   a. *Buy and Sell.* To buy, sell, mortgage, give options, or other-
      wise deal in any way in any real or personal property upon
      such items as my agent considers proper, including the
      power to buy United States Treasury Bonds that may be
      redeemed at par for the payment of federal estate tax and to
      sell or transfer Treasury securities;

   b. *Collect and Manage.* To collect, hold, maintain, improve,
      invest, lease, or otherwise manage any or all of my real or
      personal property;

   c. *Business and Banking.* To conduct and participate in any lawful
      business activity including the right to continue, reorganize,
      merge, consolidate, recapitalize, close, liquidate, sell, or dis-
      solve any business and to vote stock, including the exercise of
      any stock options and the carrying out of any buy-sell agree-
      ment; to receive and endorse checks and other negotiable
      papers, deposit and withdraw funds (by check or withdrawal
      slip) in or from any bank, savings and loan, or other
      institution;

   d. *Life Insurance.* To exercise incidents of ownership, other than
      to change the beneficiary, with respect to policies of life in-
      surance, except policies insuring the life of my agent;

   e. *Government Benefits.* To make application to any governmental
      agency for any benefit or government obligation to which I
      may be entitled;

   f. *Legal Proceedings.* To engage in any administrative or legal
      proceedings or in any litigation in connection with the pre-
      mises, including litigation to enforce this power of attorney;

g. *Borrow.* To borrow money, execute promissory notes, and secure the obligation by mortgage or pledge of assets;

h. *Act as Agent.* To act as my agent or proxy in respect to any stocks, bonds, shares, or other investments, rights, or interests;

i. *Delegation of Authority.* To engage and dismiss agents, counsel, and employees, and to appoint and remove at pleasure any substitute for my agent, in connection with any matter, upon such terms as my agent shall think fit;

j. *Tax Returns.* To prepare, execute, and file income and other tax returns, and other governmental reports and documents, and to represent me in all matters before the Internal Revenue Service, and in connection with any matter or controversy with the Internal Revenue Service, to execute their form 2848 (or substitute) authorizing my agent or another to act on my behalf with respect to a particular tax or taxes for the years indicated;

k. *Transfers in Trust.* To transfer any interest I may have in property, real or personal, to the trustee of any trust created by me for my benefit;

l. *Safe Deposit Boxes.* To have access to any safety deposit box registered in my name alone or jointly with others;

m. *Disclaimers.* To disclaim property, interests in property, or powers to which I may become entitled; and

n. *Gifts.* To make gifts from my assets when authorized by an order of a court having jurisdiction over my assets that finds that the gift is within the scope of my desires (expressed in a prior gift program, in my estate plan, or otherwise) and that it does not jeopardize my economic security.

4. *Restrictions on Agent's Powers.* Regardless of the above statements, my agent shall not exercise any powers that would cause my assets to be taxable to my agent or in my agent's estate for any income, estate, or inheritance tax.

5. *Obligations and Liabilities.* Third parties may rely upon the representation of my agent as to all matters relating to any power granted to my agent, and no person who may act in reliance upon the representations of my agent or the authority granted to my agent shall incur any liability to me or my estate as a result of permitting my agent to exercise any power. For the purpose of inducing third parties to rely on this power of attorney, I warrant that, if this power of attorney is revoked by me or otherwise terminated, I will indemnify and save the third party harmless from any loss suffered or liability incurred by the third party in good-faith reliance on the authority of my agent prior to the third party's actual knowledge of revocation or termination of this power of attorney, whether such termination is by operation of law or otherwise.

6. *Disability.* This power shall continue to be effective even if I am disabled.

7. *Counterparts.* Reproductions of this executed original (with reproduced signatures) shall be deemed to be original counterparts of this power of attorney.

Dated: _____   /s/ _____

Signed in the presence of:

/s/ _____   /s/ _____
Witness   Witness

Subscribed and sworn to before me on

_____ .

/s/ _____
Notary Public, _____ County
My commission expires _____

sell them in your absence and may, if the trustee has been carefully selected, be able to increase the value of the trust estate far more rapidly than you could by yourself. These advantages may be well worth your loss of some degree of control.

VULNERABILITY TO CREDITORS AND OTHER CLAIMANTS

If you are at any time unable to pay your personal debts, any property that you own individually is subject to the claims of your creditors. This means that except for certain exempt assets, anything of value that you own can legally be seized not only by merchants whose bills you have not paid but also by a bankruptcy trustee, by government authorities if you are delinquent in your tax payments, or by anyone who has obtained a judgment against you for damages beyond the limits of your liability insurance coverage. If, however, your property is in joint ownership (see Chap. 3) or is owned by some form of trust (see Chap. 4) or by your closely held corporation (see Chap. 5), it may be partly or completely insulated from any of these claimants for the simple reason that it does not belong to you alone.

Shifting your assets out of sole ownership into an alternative form does not, of course, give you license to ignore your legitimate debts. In fact, the deliberate transfer of assets into another form of ownership or to another person to avoid paying your debts is known as a *fraudulent conveyance* and may be reversible by your creditors. But in many circumstances joint, trust, or corporate ownership may offer you breathing space during a financial crisis and may possibly protect you against disaster if a court should assess an astronomical money damage claim against you.

STATE AND FEDERAL INCOME TAXES

State and federal income taxes on the yield from or the sale of any property you own are, of course, payable by you, even if you use the money for the benefit of others. Suppose, for example, that you are setting aside money for a child's college education and that you have accumulated $20,000 in a money market account registered in your own name. If its current annual yield is $1,000 and you are in the 31% tax bracket, you will pay $310 in federal income tax plus any state income or "intangibles" tax. If, instead, you had opened the account as a Custodial Account for Minors (see Chap. 4), your child may be liable for the income tax, and if he or she had no other income, would pay no tax at all.

Even transferring solely owned property into joint tenancy (see Chap. 3) can sometimes result in a tax reduction because the tax liability on its yield is shared by the co-owners. If the joint tenant is your spouse and you file a joint return, you are unlikely to enjoy any tax reduction, but joint ownership can involve more than two owners and in certain circumstances there may be no reason why one of them should not be an adult child, who is likely to be in a lower income bracket than you or your spouse.

PROBATE

A severe disadvantage of sole ownership often becomes apparent only after the owner dies, and perhaps this is why many people remain unaware of it or are reluctant to confront it. Although sole ownership would seem to give you the right to bequeath anything you own to anyone you choose, there are, in reality, significant restrictions on this right, and the state's enforcement of these restrictions through the probate court can turn out to be extremely costly to your estate and frustrating and time-consuming to your surviving beneficiaries.

Generally speaking, there are no restrictions on your bequeathing to anyone you choose items of personal property that are not formally registered or titled in your name and that have only moderate value. You have every right, for example, to leave a favorite shotgun to a hunting companion or a watch to your grandson, just as you can make these gifts during your lifetime. And normally your other personal possessions—your household furnishings, stamp collection, or jewelry, for example—will pass informally to your closest relatives, although if there is a dispute about them the contestants may need to petition the local probate court to resolve it.

But items of substantial value that are titled in your name alone—your house, your securities, your bank or brokerage account—cannot be transferred through use of a will to your chosen beneficiaries without being administered by the probate court or what in some states is called the surrogate, chancery, or orphans' court.

The probating of an estate is almost invariably a long-drawn-out, exasperating, and expensive process, but its fundamental purpose is one that most people would approve of. It is society's way of ensuring that on your death the interests of other people—your family, your creditors, and the tax authorities—will be protected. This is why none of your solely owned assets can be passed to your survivors until your local probate court has made certain that any document purporting to be your will was properly executed and proven, that you have not completely disinherited your spouse, that all your creditors' lawful claims have been satisfied and any income or death taxes you owe have been paid, and that your assets are fairly distributed to your designated beneficiaries or your heirs at law. If you should die without a will, the probate process will identify the individuals whom the law specifies as your "heirs at law" and will divide and distribute your estate's probate assets among them.

The probate court exercises its responsibility by appointing a *personal representative* (sometimes called an executor or administrator) whom it authorizes to inventory, appraise, and liquidate your assets; to notify your creditors; to pay your bills and your taxes; and, ultimately, to distribute the residue of your solely owned (probate) assets to your beneficiaries in accordance with the provisions of your will or, if you left no will, to your heirs at law.

The personal representative is entitled to a fee for his work, and he must usually be bonded to protect your estate against his possible negligence or fraud. In addition, the personal representative is authorized to hire lawyers, accountants, realtors, appraisers, and others to help in settling the estate. Because all these costs, plus court fees, death taxes, and other expenses, are payable by your estate, it is easy to see that the probate process can significantly erode the value of the estate before it is distributed to your survivors.

The probate process is costly in terms of time as well as money. The probating of a relatively simple estate usually takes at least six months; a complex estate may take several years. This can create serious problems for your survivors if they urgently need some of the assets you have left them.

You can avoid the probate process if you bear in mind that the only assets subject to it are those that, at the time of your death, are titled *in your own name alone.* Since you obviously have no right to bequeath by will anything you do not own individually, anything that you own jointly (see Chap. 3) or that you have placed in some form of trust (see Chap. 4) is not subject to probate administration.

This does not imply that you should immediately shift absolutely everything you possess from sole ownership to some form that exempts it from the probate process. In order to reduce the problems of probate for people with limited assets, almost every state has adopted some form of "small estate" transfer procedure that is swift, informal, and inexpensive (see Tables 1 and 2). Hence, there is no reason why you should not retain in sole ownership, if you like, assets whose value does not exceed the maximum permitted by the small estate procedures of your state. In addition, there are some assets that you probably should retain in sole ownership even at the risk of probate. These are discussed in the last section of this chapter.

But if your assets substantially exceed your state's small estate limits, and if you are concerned about the inevitable costs, delays, and frustrations of the probate process, you may want to consider shifting some of your assets into one of the forms of ownership described in Chapters 3 and 4, all of which promise the quick and easy transfer of the assets to your designated beneficiaries without the costs and delays of probate.

FEDERAL GIFT AND ESTATE TAXES

In addition to taxing your income as you receive it, the federal government also imposes a tax on your outgo—assets that you give away during your lifetime or pass on after your death. Unlike the

Table 1
STATE REQUIREMENTS FOR SMALL ESTATE TRANSFER
BY AFFIDAVIT

State	Dollar Limitation ($)	Waiting Period Following Death	Procedure Excludes Real Estate	Creditors Must First Be Paid
Alabama		Not available		
Alaska[1]	15,000	30 days	Yes	No
Arizona[1]	30,000	30	Yes	Yes
Arkansas[1]	50,000	45	Yes	Yes
California	60,000	40	Yes	No
Colorado[1]	27,000	10	Yes	No
Connecticut[1]	20,000	30	Yes	Yes
Delaware[1]	12,500	30	Yes	Yes
District of Columbia		Not available		
Florida		Not available		
Georgia		Not available		
Hawaii[1]	5,000	30	Yes	No
Idaho[1]	5,000	30	Yes	No
Illinois	25,000	No	Yes	Yes
Indiana[1]	15,000	45	Yes	No
Iowa		Not available		
Kansas		Not available		
Kentucky		Not available		
Louisiana[3]	50,000	No	Yes	Yes
Maine[1]	10,000	30	Yes	No
Maryland	Formula[4]	No	Yes	Yes
Massachusetts	Formula[5]	60	Yes	No
Michigan[1]	5,000	No	Yes	No
Minnesota	10,000	30	Yes	No
Mississippi	20,000	30	Yes	No
Missouri	15,000	30	No	Yes
Montana[1]	7,500	30	Yes	No
Nebraska	10,000	30	Yes	No
Nevada	10,000	30	Yes	No
New Hampshire[2,7]	500	No	Yes	No
New Jersey[2,3]	10,000	No	No	No
New Mexico[1]	20,000	30	Yes	No
New York	10,000	30	Yes	No
North Carolina	10,000	30	Yes	Yes
North Dakota[1]	15,000	30	Yes	No
Ohio[7]	2,500	No	Yes	No
Oklahoma		Not available		
Oregon	60,000	30	No	Yes

(continued)

Table 1 (continued)
STATE REQUIREMENTS FOR SMALL ESTATE TRANSFER
BY AFFIDAVIT

State	Dollar Limitation ($)	Waiting Period Following Death	Procedure Excludes Real Estate	Creditors Must First Be Paid
Pennsylvania		Not available		
Rhode Island[1]	7,500	45	Yes	No[6]
South Carolina	10,000	30	Yes	No
South Dakota	10,000	No	Yes	Yes
Tennessee	1,000	30	Yes	No
Texas		Not available		
Utah[1]	25,000	30	Yes	No
Vermont		Not available		
Virginia	5,000	60	Yes	No
Washington	30,000	40	Yes	Yes
West Virginia[7]	1,000	120	Yes	No
Wisconsin	10,000	No	Yes	No
Wyoming[1]	70,000	30	Yes	Yes

[1]Not available if petition for appointment of personal representative has been granted or is pending.

[2]Available only if deceased is survived by a spouse.

[3]Available only if deceased left no will.

[4]Not more than two vehicles plus a boat (maximum value of $5,000) plus life insurance (maximum value of $1,000).

[5]Life insurance up to $2,000 plus bank accounts up to $3,000 plus wages up to $100.

[6]Funeral expenses must first be paid.

[7]Available only for wages, salaries, and commissions.

federal income tax, the federal gift and estate tax affects only the most affluent taxpayers, who make up less than one percent of the population. Nevertheless, since you have no way of predicting your future net worth, you ought to be aware of this tax, because it may influence not only the form in which you own your assets but also the scheduling of any gifts you make during your lifetime.

Unlike the federal income tax, which is withheld from your earned income and is payable quarterly or annually on your unearned income, the federal estate tax involves no periodic cash payments and is, in fact, payable not by you but by your estate after your death. Instead of collecting the tax on a pay-as-you-go basis, the federal government offers you a lifetime exemption in the form of a "line of credit" against which you can charge (1) taxable gifts you making during your lifetime and (2) the value of your taxable estate after your death. On your death, your estate will owe no taxes

Table 2
STATE REQUIREMENTS FOR SMALL ESTATE SUMMARY
PROBATE PROCEDURE

State	Dollar Limitation ($)	Waiting Period Following Death	Procedure Excludes Real Estate	Creditors Must First Be Paid
Alabama	3,000	No	Yes	Yes
Alaska	Formula[2]	No	No	No
Arizona	Formula[2]	No	No	No
Arkansas	Formula[3]	No	Yes	No
California	60,000	No	No	No
Colorado	Formula[2]	No	No	No
Connecticut		Not available		
Delaware		Not available		
District of Columbia	10,000	No	No	No
Florida	60,000	No	No	Yes
Georgia		Not available		
Hawaii	20,000	No	No	No
Idaho	Formula[2]	No	No	No
Illinois[5]	50,000[4]	No	No	Yes
Indiana	Formula[2]	No	No	No
Iowa[6]	50,000	No	No	Yes
Kansas	Formula[2]	6 mos.	No	Yes
Kentucky[5 or 7]	7,500	No	No	Yes
Louisiana		Not available		
Maine	Formula[2]	No	No	No
Maryland	20,000	30 days	Yes	Yes
Massachusetts[1]	15,000	30	Yes	No
Michigan	Formula[2]	No	No	No
Minnesota[1, 8]	30,000	No	No	No
Mississippi		Not available		
Missouri	Formula[2]	No	No	No
Montana	Formula[2]	No	No	No
Nebraska	Formula[2]	No	No	No
Nevada	100,000	60	No	Yes
New Hampshire	5,000	No	No	Yes
New Jersey		Not available		
New Mexico	Formula[2]	No	No	Yes
New York[8]	10,000[9]	No	No	No
North Carolina		Not available		
North Dakota	Formula[2]	No	No	No
Ohio	25,000	No	No	Yes
Oklahoma	60,000	No	No	Yes
Oregon	Formula[2]	No	No	Yes
Pennsylvania	10,000	No	Yes	No

(continued)

Table 2 (continued)
STATE REQUIREMENTS FOR SMALL ESTATE SUMMARY PROBATE PROCEDURE

State	Dollar Limitation ($)	Waiting Period Following Death	Procedure Excludes Real Estate	Creditors Must First Be Paid
Rhode Island		Not available		
South Carolina[8]	10,000	No	No	No
South Dakota	60,000	No	No	Yes
Tennessee	10,000	45	No	Yes
Texas	50,000[9]	30	No	Yes
Utah	Formula[2]	No	No	No
Vermont	10,000	No	Yes	Yes
Virginia	5,000	60	Yes	No
Washington		Not available		
West Virginia	50,000	No	No	No
Wisconsin	30,000	No	No	Yes
Wyoming	70,000	No	No	Yes

[1]Not available if petition for appointment of personal representative has been granted or is pending.

[2]Available where entire estate, less liens and encumbrances, does not exceed certain statutory allowances plus expenses of last illness, funeral, and administration . . . all of which may approximate $25,000 in some cases.

[3]If personal property is less than statutory dower and allowances to widow or minors, court may immediately assign estate to them.

[4]Includes deceased's probate and nonprobate assets.

[5]Available only if all beneficiaries consent in writing.

[6]Available only if deceased is survived by a spouse, children, or a parent.

[7]Available only if deceased is survived by a spouse.

[8]Available only if deceased left no will.

[9]Exclusive of statutory family allowances or exempt property.

unless these two items exceed $600,000. To determine your exposure to this tax, you need to know the meaning of its two basic terms: *taxable gift* and *taxable estate*.

Taxable Gift

A taxable gift, one that must be charged against your exemption, is (1) any gift of more than $3,000 (or $6,000 if made with the consent of your spouse) that you made in any one year before 1982 and (2) any gift of more than $10,000 (or $20,000 with the consent of your spouse) made in any year after 1981. If you make one or more such gifts, you must file a federal gift tax return so that the IRS can charge them against your lifetime exemption.

Gifts to a spouse are exempt from these limits, and so is each gift to others so long as its value does not exceed the annual exemption limits. Moreover, because these limits are based on a calendar year, you can make nontaxable gifts of $10,000/$20,000 to a child or to anyone else on December 31 and duplicate it on January 1 of the following year with no effect on your lifetime exemption. If you exceed your annual exemption of $10,000/$20,000 per recipient, you must file a federal gift tax return, even though no tax will be payable until you exceed your lifetime exemption — either during your lifetime or after your death, when the value of your taxable estate must be determined.

Taxable Estate

Your taxable estate is not necessarily equivalent in value to your probate estate, because, as Table 3 indicates, the IRS includes in its calculations not only all your probate assets but also your share of any jointly held assets, any assets held in a revocable trust established by you, the proceeds of your life insurance (if you owned the policies or assigned them within three years of your death), and various other assets.

You are, however, allowed certain deductions. The most important of these is the unlimited marital deduction, which permits you to leave your entire estate to your surviving spouse free of any federal estate tax. Other deductions include funeral and burial expenses, the medical costs of a terminal illness, the costs of administering your estate, and any unpaid debts or mortgages.

Briefly, the value of your estate for federal estate tax purposes is determined by the following formula: GROSS VALUE OF THE ESTATE (the sum of all items in Table 3) − DEDUCTIONS = ADJUSTED GROSS ESTATE − UNLIMITED MARITAL DEDUCTION AND CHARITABLE GIFTS = TAXABLE ESTATE.

An obvious way for an individual owner to avoid the federal estate tax altogether is to leave everything to his or her spouse. But this can create serious problems because the surviving spouse will be left with substantial assets, all of them in his or her own name and, hence, all probatable unless transferred into some other form of ownership. In addition, unless the surviving spouse remarries, he or she will not be able, in turn, to take advantage of the unlimited marital deduction and may consequently leave an estate large enough to be taxable.

Table 3
LEGAL CONSEQUENCES OF VARIOUS FORMS OF OWNERSHIP

| Form of ownership | Subject to | | Control during your lifetime | Bequeathable by will | Subject to creditors' claims | | After-death availability to beneficiaries |
	Probate	Federal estate tax			Before death	After death	
Asset solely owned	Yes	All	Full	Yes	Yes	Yes	Delayed
Asset owned jointly by spouses	No[1]	One-half	Divided	No[1]	Yes	No[2]	Immediate[1]
Asset owned jointly by nonspouses	No[1]	All[3]	Divided	No[1]	Yes	No[1]	Immediate[1]
Assets in bank account (Totten) trust	No	All	Full	No	Yes	No	Immediate
Assets in custodial account for minors	No	None[4]	Limited	No	No	No	Immediate
Life insurance owned by insured	No[6]	All	Full	No[6]	No	No[6]	Immediate
Life insurance owned by other than insured	No[6]	None[8]	None	No	No	No[6]	Immediate
Life insurance payable to deceased's estate	Yes	All	Full	Yes	Yes[7]	Yes	Delayed
Assets in a revocable living trust	No	All	Full	No	Yes	No[9]	Immediate[5]

Assets in an irrevocable living trust	No	None	None	No	No	No	Immediate[5]

[1] Provided that you are survived by a joint owner.

[2] Unless debt was incurred by both joint owners.

[3] Except to the extent your estate can prove that a surviving joint owner contributed to the acquisition or improvement of the asset.

[4] Unless you are a custodian as well as a donor.

[5] Subject, however, to all of the terms of the trust, which may include a provision postponing distribution of the asset.

[6] Provided that you are survived by a beneficiary designated in the insurance policy. Otherwise the proceeds become a part of your probate estate.

[7] Limited to the cash surrender value of the policy.

[8] Unless you assigned the policy to another within three years of the date of your death.

[9] Some states have recently adopted laws permitting creditors, after death, to satisfy their claims from assets left in the deceased's revocable living trust.

During most of your life, one way to reduce your estate's eventual liability for any federal estate tax is to reduce its value gradually and in affordable amounts by giving your assets away, not only by way of philanthropic gifts but by gifts to family members, especially your children. Custodial accounts, trust for minors, and certain other types of trusts (see Chap. 4) reduce an estate's exposure to federal taxes at your death; they also reduce exposure to state and federal income taxes during your lifetime.

A far more effective device for avoiding the tax is to transfer assets into an irrevocable trust (see Chap. 4) at the rate of $10,000/$20,000 or less annually. Although this is likely to be impracticable for most people in their early and middle years, it can be a useful tactic in the latter part of life.

One item that usually is not probatable but is subject to federal estate tax is the proceeds of any life insurance policies on your own life. You can insulate these proceeds against taxation by the simple expedient or assigning your life insurance policies to someone else, usually the primary beneficiary. The assignment procedure involves nothing more than filling out a form available from your insurance agent or the company's home office. This tactic will not avoid the tax, however, should you die within three years of making the assignment. Furthermore, assignment constitutes a gift of a life insurance policy and may be subject to federal gift tax if the *current cash surrender* value of the policy exceeds $10,000/$20,000. Term insurance policies, however, have no cash value at any time.

Because the recipient of your policy becomes responsible for all premiums and has the right to change beneficiaries and to cash in or borrow against the policy at any time, this kind of transfer should be made only to someone in whom you have a high degree of trust and confidence.

WHAT YOU SHOULD RETAIN
IN SOLE OWNERSHIP

Having considered the disadvantages and limitations of sole ownership, you may be tempted to move the bulk of your assets immediately into one of the alternative forms described in the chapters that follow. But before doing this you need to evaluate your family situation thoughtfully and cautiously.

To begin with, some of the alternative forms—joint ownership, custodial accounts, and certain types of trusts, for example—are virtually or totally irrevocable. Once you establish them, your control and use of the assets may either diminish or evaporate entirely. Hence, you should only transfer ownership to or share it with people with whom you are likely to have a very stable relationship. If you feel that there is even a remote possibility that your marriage will end in divorce, joint ownership with your spouse presents obvious risks.

Secondly, you need to recognize that shifting assets to a different form of ownership is not an all-or-nothing procedure. You have the right to use several of the alternatives rather than just one, and you should assess their advantages to find the most useful way to own each of your major assets.

You may decide, for example, to transfer most of your assets—your house, your securities, your savings accounts—into joint ownership with your spouse. But if you do, you would be well advised to retain your automobile in sole ownership. For one thing, if you are found liable in an automobile accident and the judgment against you exceeds your insurance coverage, your jointly owned property cannot be attached to satisfy the claim nearly as easily as it could be if the automobile were jointly owned. In addition, most states permit the transfer of a solely owned motor vehicle after the owner's death to a surviving spouse or next of kin without the need for any probate administration.

Another reason for retaining sole ownership is to protect a spouse who is especially vulnerable to malpractice or negligence lawsuits. Some physicians, for example, instead of paying high premiums for malpractice insurance, choose the alternative of "going bare"—that is, they transfer most of their assets into their spouse's name—as a tax-exempt gift—and retain virtually nothing in their own in the hope that anyone contemplating a malpractice suit against them will realize that any damages awarded would not be readily collectible. (Given the high divorce rate among physicians, however, this may be a very risky tactic.)

Nevertheless, unless you are a social isolate with no relatives or friends, it is likely that you will find advantages in alternative forms of ownership for at least some of your assets. These forms are shown in Table 3 and described in the next three chapters.

CHAPTER 3

SHARING OWNERSHIP WITH OTHERS

Sharing the ownership of property with one or more other persons may strike you as a good deal less desirable than owning it all by yourself—and if the property was acquired through your own efforts and hence really "belongs" to you, sharing its ownership may strike you as downright irrational. Yet co-ownership of all sorts of real and personal property—not only homes but also bank accounts, securities, and other items of value—is quite common. Most co-owners are married couples, but many are not. Frequently ownership is shared by parents and children, grandparents and grandchildren, siblings, other relatives, friends or unmarried cohabitants.

Obviously, then, co-ownership offers—or at least promises—some very significant advantages over sole ownership. But some of these advantages are more apparent than real, some depend on the specific form of co-ownership, and many are coupled with limitations or distinct disadvantages, which may not be immediately apparent.

There are three basic forms of co-ownership: *joint tenancy, tenancy by the entirety,* and *tenancy in common,* and they differ significantly from one another. We shall deal first with joint tenancy, because its simplicity, versatility, and other advantages combine to make it by far the most popular form of co-ownership. The other two forms, discussed later in this chapter, also deserve mention, because you

27

may find them appropriate either for your personal situation or for some of your possessions. And *partnership*, essentially a special form of tenancy in common, may be suitable for your business activities. Bear in mind that co-ownership is not an all-or-nothing matter: You may decide to use different forms at different times in your life or for different assets; you may also decide to retain some assets in sole ownership.

If you live in a community property state (see Chap. 8), bear in mind also that the conditions of co-ownership will be significantly affected by the laws of those states.

JOINT TENANCY

Under joint tenancy—usually abbreviated on stock certificates and bank records as JT TEN or JT WROS—two or more persons can share the legal ownership of any kind of property: a house, cottage, office, or other real estate, bank accounts and securities, antiques, or virtually anything of value. Because each joint tenant has what is known as an "undivided interest" in the jointly owned property, either or any one of them is entitled to full use of the property and to his or her *share* of any income it may yield, regardless of which of them acquired it initially. The share of each tenant is automatically determined by the number of persons involved in the joint tenancy. If there are two tenants, each is entitled to one-half; if three, one-third; and so on.

The most significant characteristic of joint tenancy is that it includes *rights of survivorship*. That is, upon the death of any one joint tenant, his or her interest passes automatically, by operation of law, to the surviving tenant or tenants. Because property held in joint tenancy is not considered part of the deceased tenant's probate estate, it passes to the surviving tenants without the delay and expense of probate.

The Attractions of Joint Tenancy

Symbolic Significance. For couples who have just married—and, indeed, for some cohabitants who have dispensed with the formality of marriage—joint tenancy may have considerable symbolic value because it reflects, in a sense, compliance with the "with all my worldly goods I thee endow" stipulation of the Protestant marriage service. The partners may see the merging of their individual assets into joint ownership as somehow reinforcing their merger into a social and emotional partnership. And the element of automatic inheritability reflects each partner's concern for the other's future welfare. Given the current divorce rate and the difficulty of terminating a joint tenancy, this view may not be altogether rational, but it is quite common.

Convenience. Aside from its symbolic value, however, joint tenancy offers some very practical advantages, among them convenience. In many circumstances one joint tenant can act on behalf of the other(s) whenever they are unavailable. If, for example, you are traveling abroad, or are hospitalized or otherwise unavailable or incapacitated, a joint tenant can buy or sell jointly owned securities, pay bills from a joint checking account, retrieve an urgently needed document from a jointly leased safe deposit box, and in general take care of many financial concerns.

Protection Against Creditors Joint tenancy, in addition, offers protection against creditors' claims after your death. Since your jointly owned property passes automatically to your surviving joint tenant(s) and therefore is no longer yours, and since normally no person – not even your spouse – is responsible for your debts (unless you incurred them jointly), the jointly owned assets need not be used to satisfy any debts that are outstanding at the time of your death.

Protection against creditors' claims during your lifetime, however, is a different matter. If, for example, you declare bankruptcy, of if you are found culpable in an automobile accident and the damage award exceeds your liability insurance coverage, joint tenancy does not offer you complete immunity.

In such circumstances the vulnerability of jointly held assets to creditors depends on the nature of the asset and the laws of your state, but generally speaking the share of the jointly held asset that you originally contributed is likely to be vulnerable to creditors' claims. Thus, if you hold a bank account in joint tenancy with your spouse but in fact all deposits came from your earnings, your creditors may have the right to attach all of it. If, on the other hand, 50 percent of the house which you hold in joint tenancy was paid for by your joint tenant, only half its value would be available to satisfy your creditors' claims.

Creditors seeking to attach jointly held assets must first file suit and obtain a judgment against you, a process that may discourage them from trying to collect relatively small debts. Against major debts and damage claims, however, joint tenancy offers far less protection than another form of co-ownership, tenancy by the entirety, discussed later in this chapter.

Tax Advantages.   As we shall see, joint tenancy may offer certain tax advantages, but mainly with respect to death taxes—the federal gift and estate tax and the various state inheritance taxes. With respect to federal and state income taxes, the advantages are probably more limited than many people believe.

Inheritability.   One indisputable advantage of joint tenancy undoubtedly accounts for its enormous popularity with spouses, other family members, and close friends. That is the automatic inheritability of the jointly held property by the surviving joint tenant(s). This simple and inexpensive tactic for avoiding the expense and delay of probate administration is so widely appreciated that some people place almost everything they own into joint tenancy with spouses, children, and others whom they expect to survive them. With the bulk of their assets in joint tenancy, they anticipate that the value of the few assets remaining in sole ownership upon their death will be low enough to qualify for the various types of small estate transfer procedures that avoid full probate administration (see Chap. 2). This is why joint ownership has been called "the poor man's will."

Although there is no doubt that joint ownership, carefully planned, can avoid probate or reduce its costs, it does not, as we shall see shortly, relieve you of the need to make a will or to devote further effort to estate and possibly tax planning.

Some Disadvantages of Joint Tenancy

Seduced by its obvious advantages, many people precipitately place most of their assets into joint tenancy without an awareness of its limitations. Some of these may strike you as insignificant or irrelevant to your personal situation, but others can give rise to serious problems, either immediately or in the future.

Risk.   In order to gain the advantage of convenience, both (or all) co-tenants must have unrestricted access to the jointly held assets; they must be able to sign checks, liquidate securities or other assets, and remove the contents of a safe deposit box. But with such access, there is nothing to prevent a co-tenant from liquidating and absconding with the assets at any time. This means that you should not consider as a joint tenant anyone with whom you do not anticipate a very stable relationship for the foreseeable future. Considering the fact, however, that many divorces occur between spouses in their fifties, that many children become alienated from their parents on reaching adulthood, and that many close friendships terminate unexpectedly, it is inevitable that joint tenancy involves some degree of risk.

In addition to caution in the selection of joint tenants, this risk can be reduced in other ways. Money market and bank accounts, for example, can be set up so that withdrawals require the signatures of two or more tenants rather than one. The sale of stock by one of the tenants can be prevented by having the stock certificates in your own possession rather than in your brokerage account, since stock certificates cannot be transferred without the guaranteed signature endorsement of all owners. These precautionary measures, however, not only violate the spirit of joint tenancy but also reduce the convenience that it offers.

Inflexibility.   Once established, a joint tenancy may be well-nigh impossible to modify or terminate, especially when real estate is involved. It can, of course, be terminated at any time with the consent of the tenants, and it is either terminated or modified automatically upon the death of one co-tenant, since his share immediately becomes the property of the surviving tenant(s). It also can be dissolved by a court in decreeing a divorce between the tenants or in response to a "partition" lawsuit initiated by one of the tenants asking that the property be divided or sold, with the proceeds divided. But aside from these possibilities, you should regard joint tenancy as essentially a "till death us do part" arrangement. This might be satisfactory if you could foretell the future, but most people can't do this very accurately, not only with respect to the stability of their marriage and their relationships with children who are joint tenants but also, more important, with respect to death and subsequent inheritance.

Unintended Inheritance.   Although automatic inheritability is the most attractive feature of joint tenancy, the inflexibility of this form of ownership can result in both unintended inheritance and unintended disinheritance.

Often, for example, a parent sets up joint tenancy with an adult child for the sole purpose of convenience, so that the child can manage an account with a bank, a broker, or a money market fund in the parent's temporary absence. If the parent should die unexpectedly, however, that child will automatically acquire the joint accounts, and the spouse and other children will get nothing from them. This kind of "inheritance" can be challenged by the heirs who were thus disinherited, but litigation is costly, protracted, and enormously frustrating. Although the problem can be averted by a written agreement, signed by both parent and child, stipulating that no inheritance is intended, a far simpler option would be for the parent to avoid joint tenancy and, instead, give the child a power of attorney to deal with the accounts. (See Chap. 2.)

Joint tenancy can also result in disinheritance of children of prior marriages. If, for example, you remarry after the death or divorce of a spouse and you place your assets in joint tenancy with your new spouse, the children of your first marriage will inherit nothing if you predecease your spouse—an outcome you may not have intended.

But the most significant limitation of automatic inheritability stems from the fact that no one can predict which tenant will die first. Suppose that an elderly widow places her house in joint tenancy with her son, intending that he acquire it automatically on her death without the necessity of probate. If the son should die before she does, sole ownership of the house would remain with her, upon her death, it would become part of her probate estate. On the other hand, if she places the house in joint tenancy with her son and her daughter and the son dies first, on her own death ownership of the house would pass automatically to her daughter, and the son's children would receive no share of this asset.

All of these unintended consequences can be averted if, instead of joint tenancy, you utilize a revocable living trust. As we shall see in the next chapter, this form of ownership provides automatic inheritability but can always be altered with respect to the property involved, the designation of trustees and beneficiaries, and other circumstances that are subject to change.

As an alternative to joint ownership of bank accounts and securities, most states authorize use of payable-on-death (POD) or transfer-on-death (TOD) beneficiary designations to achieve nonprobate transfers on death. Bank account depositors can designate a POD beneficiary and securities owners can specify a TOD beneficiary. Such a beneficiary, although having no access or control during the owner's lifetime, will acquire the bank account balance or the securities after the owner's death, free of probate administration. These provisions are found in the Uniform Nonprobate Transfers On Death Act (adopted by 12 states), in some versions of the Uniform Probate Code, and in separate laws enacted by several states.

The Avoidance of Probate

The automatic inheritability feature of jointly owned property leads many people to conclude that they need not write a will. But there are at least two reasons why joint tenancy does not relieve one of this responsibility.

To begin with, you can never be certain that all your assets will be in joint tenancy at the time of your death. Almost inevitably your estate will include some property that remains solely owned, because it could not or should not have been placed in joint tenancy or because your joint tenant predeceased you. Unless you have left a will, this property will be distributed by the probate court to your "heirs at law" specified by state law, and these persons may not be the same individuals you would have chosen as your beneficiaries.

A properly drawn will becomes especially important in the event that you and your joint owner(s) die together in an automobile accident, a plane crash, or some other unforeseeable common disaster. Under the Uniform Simultaneous Death Act, adopted by all states, if your deaths are simultaneous, *each* of you is assumed to have survived the other and, hence, half of all your jointly owned assets will be regarded as belonging to each of you. This means that each of your estates will be subject to the expense and delay of probate administration and that, in the absence of a will, they may be distributed to each joint owner's heirs as determined by state law.

In case of the simultaneous deaths of joint tenants, the separate probate administration of each tenant's estate can be prevented if both wills contain a "common disaster clause," an example of which follows:

> In the event that my wife and I die simultaneously or under circum-
> stances where it cannot be determined who died first, then it shall be
> presumed that [I survived my wife],* and all provisions of my will shall
> be construed based upon such presumption.

Because it specifies the predecease of one spouse (and hence automatic inheritance of jointly held property by the survivor), such

---

*The wife's will should, of course, specify that "my husband survived me." Usually the husband should be designated as the survivor because he is likely to have more probatable assets than the wife and hence his estate is more likely to require probate, but the choice of survivor should depend on individual circumstances.

a clause avoids double probate and the consequences of the Uniform Simultaneous Death Act, but it points up another limitation of joint tenancy, one that is unrelated to simultaneous death. Upon the death of the first of two joint owners, the survivor will be deprived of the probate-avoidance advantage unless he or she immediately established joint ownership with a new co-tenant—perhaps a son or daughter or someone else to whom the survivor plans to bequeath the property—or chooses some other arrangement that avoids probate. Establishing a new joint tenancy is simple enough, but it is often overlooked or neglected, especially by elderly widows or widowers after the death of a mate.

Establishing Joint Tenancy

As we have noted, joint ownership can be used for any type of asset and can involve any number of tenants. The tenants need not share a common residence or even live in the same state, but in some circumstances they need to record their signatures when the tenancy is established and to be available for a signature endorsement when assets are sold or transferred.

Designating a minor child as a joint owner is not illegal, but it can create problems in some circumstances. Since minors are not legally capable of selling real estate, stocks, or other types of assets, the sale of a house or stock certificates owned in joint tenancy with a minor may require the appointment of a guardian or a conservator. There is no such restriction with respect to bank accounts, but most parents who consider joint tenancy of a bank account with one or more minor children would find a custodial account, a Totten trust, or a formal revocable trust a far more advantageous arrangement. All of these are discussed in Chapter 4.

For many kinds of assets, joint tenancy is easy to set up. For securities, you need only instruct the broker to register the account in the names of all tenants and to add the notation JT TEN, which, in securities transactions, establishes rights of survivorship. Bank and money market accounts can be registered in the same way, but on these accounts it is crucially important to make sure that the account specifies rights of survivorship. In fact, you may request that the registration of the account read "as joint tenants with rights of survivorship and not as tenants in common."

To transfer real estate into joint ownership, you need only prepare and sign a new deed (see Figure 2) and record it with the county

Figure 2
REAL ESTATE DEED

KNOW ALL MEN BY THESE PRESENTS: That

whose address is

Quit Claim(s) to

whose address is

the following described premises situated in the   of

County of   and State of Michigan, to-wit:

for the full consideration of

Dated this   day of   19

         Witnesses: Signed and Sealed:

_____   _____(L.S.)

_____   _____(L.S.)

         _____(L.S.)

STATE OF MICHIGAN

COUNTY OF _____ } ss.   _____(L.S.)

The foregoing instrument was acknowledged before me this   day of   19

by

My commission expires

_____

Instrument   Notary Public_____County, Michigan

Drafted by_____   Business

      Address _____

Recording Fee_____   When recorded return to_____

State Transfer Tax _____   _____

      Send subsequent tax bills

      to _____

Tax Parcel # _____   _____

register of deeds. Motor vehicles can be transferred from individual ownership into joint tenancy by the regular transfer-of-ownership procedure required by the state department of motor vehicles, after which the joint tenancy will be specified on the vehicle's certificate of title. As we explained at the end of Chapter 2, however, it is usually advisable to retain a vehicle in sole ownership so as to limit one's exposure to liability.

When other kinds of personal property are acquired, a receipt or a bill of sale is commonly involved; if joint tenancy of the property is intended, this document should specify that the co-owners are "joint tenants and not tenants in common." Lacking such documentation, co-owners intending joint tenancy should, on acquiring the asset, state their intention in writing and preserve it with their other important papers. Figure 3 is an example of a document sufficient to establish joint tenancy.

Tax Consequences

Income Taxes, State and Federal. The assessment of taxes on the income or sale of jointly owned property is arbitrary, to say the least. As a general rule, since each joint tenant owns an equal share of an income-producing asset, each is responsible for paying income taxes on the income from his share. But as Table 4 indicates, there are exceptions to this rule, in which tax liability is based not on the share owned by each tenant but on his proportional contribution to the acquisition of the asset. For example, income produced by real estate is taxed on an equal-share basis, that from savings bonds on a proportionate contribution basis. If a father and son own a commercial property as joint tenants, each pays tax on half of the resulting income and on half the capital gain that may result when the property is sold, regardless of their respective contributions to its purchase. On the other hand, if they own U.S. Savings Bonds jointly but the father provided all the money with which they were bought, it is the father who is responsible for paying the tax on their total yield.

Tax liability for the interest on bank accounts depends on the law of the state in which the bank is located. Some states calculate each tenant's tax liability on an equal-share basis, others on the basis of each tenant's proportional contribution to the account, despite the virtual impossibility of determining each tenant's contributions to a very active account. The IRS follows state law in assessing tax liability for bank account interest.

Figure 3
ASSIGNMENT OF PERSONAL PROPERTY

The undersigned John Doe and Mary Doe (Assignors), whose address is 101 Main Street, Lansing, MI 48823, hereby assign, grant, and transfer to John Doe and Mary Doe, Husband and Wife, as joint tenants with rights of survivorship, all of Assignors' right, title, and interest in and to the following described personal property:

    (a) All of the household furnishings, appliances, equipment, tools, books, collectibles, artwork, and all other items of tangible personal property now and hereafter located at or contained in Assignors' dwelling at 101 Main St, Lansing, MI, and any other dwelling occupied by Assignors; and

    (b) All of the contents now and hereafter contained in Assignors' safe deposit box at First of America Bank, and any other safe deposit box leased to Assignors or either of them.

Date :_____

_____
John Doe, Assignor

_____
Mary Doe, Assignor

WITNESSES:

_____

_____

When securities are registered in the names of joint tenants, each tenant is taxed on his proportional share of dividends or capital gains or losses regardless of the source of funds used to buy the securities. If, however, the jointly held securities are registered in a broker's "street" account, the tax liability of each joint tenant is governed by state law, which should be consulted.

Obviously, then, whether or not joint tenancy offers an advantage with respect to income taxes depends both on the nature of the asset

Table 4
INCOME AND GIFT TAX LIABILITY FOR JOINTLY OWNED
PROPERTY

| Type | Income Tax | | Federal Gift Tax |
	By proportion of contribution	By equal shares	Gift occurs
Bank accounts	Governed by state law		When noncontributing tenant withdraws funds
U.S. Savings Bonds	X		When tenancy terminates
Securities			
registered		X	Immediately
in broker's account	Governed by state law		When tenancy terminates
Real estate		X	Immediately

and on your relationship with the joint tenant. In general, no matter whether tax is assessed on a contribution basis or a share basis, husband and wife will derive no tax advantage from joint ownershp as long as they file joint tax returns, although there may be some advantage if they file separately. Joint ownership between a father and an adult child who is in a lower tax bracket can yield a tax advantage in connection with real estate or registered securities, since the child will pay less tax on his half share, whether or not he contributed to the purchase.

Many parents assume that they can reduce or avoid income tax by setting up a joint bank or money market account with a lower-tax-bracket child who contributes nothing to the account but his name. By furnishing the financial institution with the child's taxpayer identification number (usually his Social Security number), they assume that the institution will identify all earnings from the account as belonging to the child. In fact, this tactic does not relieve the parent of any obligation for paying tax on half the yield in states that use the share basis, or on all the yield in states that assess on the basis of proportional contribution. If, however, the parent makes a gift of all or part of the account funds to the child and the child then deposits this gift in a joint account with the parent, the child has become a bona fide contributor to the account and can assume responsibility for some or all of the tax.

When a surviving joint owner sells assets of which he or she has become sole owner, special rules apply in determining gain or loss for income tax purposes. As with any gain or loss, the seller's "cost basis" must be determined; usually it is the actual cost of, or price paid for, the property. The "cost" of any property included in the deceased's taxable estate, however, is calculated on a "stepped-up" basis—its market value on the date of death, or, optionally, six months thereafter. Thus, if at the time of death the deceased was one of two joint owners of 100 shares of stock, half of the 100 shares would be valued at the stepped-up cost basis and not at the price he originally paid.

Suppose, for example, that you purchase stock for $4,000 and register it in joint ownership with your daughter. On your death, this stock is, like all property jointly owned by non-spouses, fully taxable to your estate at its then current value. So, if on your death its value has increased to $8,000 and your daughter subsequently sells it for $10,000, her taxable gain is only $2,000, because her stepped-up cost basis was $8,000, not the stock's original cost of $4,000.

On the other hand, if you and your wife buy a house for $70,000, which on your death is worth $120,000, only half of its value would be included in your taxable estate, and your spouse's stepped-up cost basis would be applicable to that half only. Thus, her cost basis would be the sum of the original cost of her share ($35,000) and the value of the share included in your taxable estate ($60,000). If she then sells the house for $120,000, her taxable gain is $25,000—unless she has not yet used the one-time exemption available to persons over the age of 54 with respect to capital gains on the sale of a primary dwelling.

If, however, you had retained the house in your own name and transferred it to her through your will (and hence through probate) or by use of a revocable living trust, its full value of $120,000 would have been included in your taxable estate and thus available to her on a stepped-up basis. A subsequent sale at this price would not result in a taxable gain.

If, therefore, you own assets that have appreciated substantially, you should balance two considerations carefully: (1) the advantages of retaining the assets in your own name, thus giving your survivors the benefit of a full stepped-up tax basis and a consequent saving of capital gains tax and (2) the advantages of joint ownership and the disadvantages of probate and possibly higher estate tax.

Federal Gift Tax. As we have noted, any gift of more than $10,000 (or $20,000 with a spouse's consent) may subject the donor to federal gift tax (which need not be paid until the donor's death). Whether the establishment of a joint tenancy gives rise to any gift tax liability, however, depends on the respective contributions of each tenant, the relationship between the tenants, and the nature of the asset.

If two persons set up a joint tenancy to which each contributes an equal amount, no gift has been made and no tax liability is incurred. If two spouses set up a joint tenancy and only one of them has contributed to it, a gift amounting to half of the value of the joint property has occurred, but no gift tax is payable because the law provides an unlimited marital deduction for gifts between spouses. Thus, the husband who, upon marriage, transfers his house or his securities portfolio into joint tenancy with his wife has made her a gift, but the gift is not subject to any gift tax.

When the respective contributions of two tenants are unequal and the tenants are not spouses, the question of whether a gift has been made and whether it is subject to federal gift tax depends on the nature of the jointly owned asset. If, for example, a parent is the sole contributor to a joint bank account with a child, no gift has been made until the child actually withdraws funds from the account. A gift occurs once the child withdraws the money, but if he withdraws at a rate of less than $10,000 a year (or $20,000 with consent of the parent's spouse), the gift will not be taxable. There is no reason why the child cannot withdraw money from time to time and immediately redeposit it in order to avoid gift tax and to assume some of the income tax liability for interest earned by the account, presumably at a lower tax rate.

The rule governing bank accounts applies also to U.S. Savings Bonds. When bonds are registered jointly, no gift is deemed to have occurred until the noncontributing tenant re-registers the bonds in his or her own name.

Securities are a different matter. If the securities are simply held in joint tenancy in a broker's street account, no gift has occurred. But if a parent *registers* the securities in joint tenancy with a child, a gift of half of the securities has occurred, because in theory, the child has a right to liquidate his or her share of the securities immediately. In such a situation a gift tax can be avoided by transferring once a year into a joint tenancy securities worth less than $20,000/$40,000 (since only half of this value will be viewed as a gift).

Jointly owned real estate is governed by the same rule as registered securities: a gift occurs at the moment that the joint tenancy is established. As in the case of registered securities, this is because the noncontributing joint owner has the right to sell his or her share of the jointly held asset.

For most people the tax consequences of making a gift are probably less significant than they may appear because the mere fact that a gift has been made does not mean that gift tax is payable. Gifts of any amount between spouses and gifts of less than $10,000/$20,000 per year to nonspouses are tax exempt. Even on taxable gifts, the unified gift and estate tax credit (see p. 18) has been so liberalized that only the very affluent are likely to pay gift tax.

Federal and State Death Taxes. The IRS treatment of jointly held property for estate-tax purposes is somewhat complex. As we have indicated earlier, property held in joint tenancy passes automatically to the surviving joint tenant(s) on the death of the first tenant and should, logically, not be considered part of the deceased's estate. But this is not true for estate tax purposes. In order to avoid loss of revenue, the IRS regards the *full value* of all jointly held property as part of the deceased's taxable estate. However, there are three important exceptions to this general rule.

First, if the surviving joint tenant is a spouse of the deceased, only one-half of the jointly held assets will be counted as part of the deceased's taxable estate and, because of the unlimited marital deduction, even that half will not be taxed.

Second, if the surviving joint tenant who is not a spouse can prove that he or she bought the jointly held asset or contributed to its acquisition or improvement, the proportion contributed will be excluded from the deceased's taxable estate.

Third, if the jointly held property was originally given or bequeathed to the joint tenants, only the deceased tenant's share will be included in his estate for tax purposes.

Many people believe that, because joint tenancy usually avoids probate, it also avoids the federal estate tax. This is not true. Unless one of the foregoing three exceptions to the general rule is applicable, the *full value* of jointly held property is included in computing potential estate-tax liability. The federal estate tax is based on the fair market value of all property included in the estate, either as of the date of death or, at the personal representative's option, six months thereafter. (The minimum value of an estate subject to this tax is $600,000.)

Given this minimum, the federal gift and estate tax is likely to affect only a small, affluent percentage of the population. But since neither your future affluence nor the rate of inflation nor the actions of future Congresses can be predicted accurately, the tax consequences of joint ownership should always be considered. Joint tenancy can, for example, result in double taxation if jointly owned property is taxed on the death of the first joint tenant and then again on the later death of the surviving tenant. The strategies for avoiding this problem will be dealt with in Chapter 4.

Almost all states have some form of death tax. On real property, this tax is payable to the state in which the property is located; tax on personal property is payable to the state in which the deceased lived, voted, and paid state income tax. State death-tax laws vary as to taxability of jointly owned property.

Terminating a Joint Tenancy

A joint tenancy can be terminated or altered in any of four ways: (1) by death of one of the tenants, (2) by an act of one of the tenants, (3) by mutual consent of all of them, and (4) by order of a court of law.

When, as is most commonly the case, a multiple joint tenancy is terminated by the death of one tenant, the surviving tenants need do nothing immediately, since they can enjoy the property and its earnings just as they did prior to the death. If, however, only two tenants were involved, the property reverts to sole ownership and the surviving tenant should promptly consider setting up a joint tenancy with a new co-tenant (if joint tenancy still seems advantageous) or using one of the alternative forms of ownership described in this and subsequent chapters.

In any event, a transfer to reflect the change in ownership should be made before the property is sold. In most cases, this involves essentially the same procedures described in connection with establishing the joint tenancy: reregistration of stock certificates and similar records and recording of death certificates and possibly new deeds or other documents affecting the title to real estate. In some states, in order to effect a transfer at death, the survivor may be required to produce a document from the state tax authority indicating that the deceased tenant's death taxes have been paid in full or that none are owed.

A joint tenancy can be terminated at any time by mutual agreement between or among the tenants. In some circumstances, however, one tenant may sell or give away his share independently. When this occurs, the new owner does not become a joint tenant. Instead, he becomes a tenant in common (see p. 45). For example, if three brothers own a piece of real estate and one of them sells his share to a stranger, the two remaining brothers retain their two-thirds interest in joint tenancy with rights of survivorship but the stranger, as a tenant in common, has no such rights.

A joint tenancy may be terminated and its assets divided between or among the tenants by a court in the course of a divorce settlement or in response to a "partition" lawsuit initiated by one of the joint tenants who is no longer interested in joint ownership. In such cases, if the property is not readily divisible the court may order that it be sold and the proceeds divided among the joint tenants.

TENANCY BY THE ENTIRETY

A hybrid form of joint ownership, tenancy by the entirety, offers two very significant advantages over joint tenancy but also has two severe limitations. First, it is recognized by only twenty-four states, and some of these restrict its use to real property only. Second, in all the states that do recognize such tenancy, it can be used only by married couples. If these limitations do not disqualify you, you may consider it in lieu of joint tenancy for at least some of your property.

Tenancy by the entirety has its roots in English common law, which held that upon marriage the two partners became an "entirety," which could hold property in its name rather than in the name of the individual partners. Tenancy by the entirety was the earliest form of co-ownership and, although it has been modified in some respects, it still retains some unique characteristics.

Like joint tenancy, tenancy by the entirety provides for automatic inheritance by the surviving spouse, but with greater certainty and finality. As we have noted, automatic inheritance by a surviving joint tenant may be challenged in the courts on grounds that it was unintended. Experience indicates, however, that inheritance by the survivor of a tenancy by the entirety is much less likely to be challenged successfully, apparently because courts feel that the tenants really intended inheritance by survivor.

More important, perhaps, tenancy by the entirety provides greater protection against the creditors of one of the co-tenants. Not only does it immunize the joint property against such claims after the death of the debtor but also, unlike joint tenancy, in many states it provides the same protection during the co-owners' lifetimes.

There are some situations in which this protection is not as useful as it may appear to be. If, for example, you apply for a personal loan, a credit card, or any other kind of credit that requires submission of a statement of net worth, and if all your assets turn out to be held in tenancy by the entirety, no sensible lender is likely to approve the loan unless it is co-signed by your spouse, in which case you get no protection because the co-signed loan is a debt for which the entirety is responsible. On the other hand, if you are sued as an individual for malpractice and the damages exceed your malpractice insurance coverage, none of your property held in tenancy by the entirety can be attached to satisfy the damage claim.

The thought may occur to you at this point that, immediately after incurring a debt or losing a lawsuit, you could protect the bulk of your assets by quickly transferring them into tenancy by the entirety. But this tactic, known as a *fraudulent conveyance,* will be of no avail if your creditors can persuade a court that you made the transfer with the intention of defrauding them.

Tax Consequences of Tenancy by the Entirety

With respect to income, gift, or estate taxes, tenancy by the entirety offers no advantages or disadvantages that distinguish it from a simple joint tenancy. The earlier discussion of the tax consequence of joint tenancy applies to tenancy by the entirety in all respects.

Establishing a Tenancy by the Entirety

In its original form, which has been retained by a number of states, tenancy by the entirety is applicable only to newly acquired property, not to property owned previously by either of the spouses or by both of them under some other form of co-ownership (see Table 3). That is, spouses may buy a new house or 100 shares of Xerox stock in tenancy by the entirety, but they are not permitted to transfer their present home, securities, or other assets into this form of ownership.

A number of states have removed this restriction, but in states that have retained it you can circumvent it by transferring any currently owned property to a third party, known as a "straw man," who will in turn transfer it back to you and your spouse as a tenancy by the entirety. You can, for example, deed your current home to an adult daughter, who can then deed it back to you and your spouse as tenants by the entirety. If, however, this back-and-forth transfer exceeds $10,000/$20,000 in value, it will be chargeable as a gift not only against your unified gift and estate tax credit but also against that of the third-party straw man.

Terminating a Tenancy by the Entirety

Like a joint tenancy, tenancy by the entirety is most commonly terminated by the death of one of the spouses, at which time ownership of the entirety's property passes to the survivor. It can also be terminated by mutual consent of the tenants. By law, a divorce terminates a tenancy by the entirety, transforming it into a tenancy in common unless other provisions are made in the divorce decree or judgment.

TENANCY IN COMMON

The third form of co-ownership, tenancy in common, is similar to joint tenancy in that it can involve two or more people, who need not be related, and it can be used for the ownership of any kind of property, real or personal, tangible or intangible. But the differences are far more important than the similarities.

The most important difference is that a tenancy in common provides no rights of survivorship. Instead, each tenant's share belongs exclusively to him. During his lifetime he has the right to sell it or give it away, and on his death his share becomes part of his probate estate instead of passing to the surviving tenant(s).

A second difference relates to the share of the asset or property owned by each tenant in common. In joint tenancy and in tenancy by the entirety, each tenant is assumed to own an equal share—that is, one-half in a tenancy by the entirety or a joint tenancy involving two tenants, or one-third in a joint tenancy involving three. In a tenancy in common, by contrast, the share owned by each tenant is clearly specified and it need bear no relationship to the number of tenants involved.

In many respects, owning something as a tenant in common is rather similar to owning 100 shares of corporate common stock. As a corporate stockholder, you own a specified share of the company, you are entitled to a specified share of the distributed profits, you have the right to sell, give away, or bequeath your shares, and you are obligated to pay tax on the income that your shares produce. Your stock is subject to claims by your creditors both before and after your death, and on your death it becomes part of your probate estate and passes not to the surviving stockholders but to your will- or trust-designated beneficiaries or to your heirs at law.

Since tenancy in common lacks the advantage of automatic inheritability and offers neither tax advantages nor protection against creditors' claims, you may wonder why we have devoted space to it. Actually, in some circumstances tenancy in common can be a very useful form of ownership, and there are various reasons why you should have some understanding of it.

For one thing, there are situations in which automatic inheritability is undesirable. Suppose, for example, that you would like your two adult children and their families to share your summer cottage after your death. If you will it to them as joint tenants or if you transfer it into joint tenancy during your lifetime and if one of them should die shortly after you do, the deceased child's share will pass automatically to the surviving sibling and the deceased child's family will have no rights to it. If, on the other hand, you will it to them as tenants in common, each can bequeath his share to his family and, in case of disagreement, the cottage can be sold and the proceeds divided.

In other situations, tenancy in common can serve as a convenient form of temporary partnership among friends, neighbors, or business associates. If, for example, a bank offers a certificate of deposit that carries a highly attractive interest rate but requires a minimum of $100,000, there is no reason why you and four friends could not each invest $20,000 and buy it as tenants in common. This kind of arrangement is useful for many kinds of investment, such as real estate, mortgages, or large blocks of stock, that are too expensive for an individual. Tenancy in common is useful, too, for a part-time enterprise—collaboration on a book, for example, or the establishment of a small home business, discussed in the section on partnership at the end of this chapter.

To cite a more modest example, if you and a neighbor would both like to own a riding lawnmower or a snowblower but hesitate to spend a considerable amount of money for something that each of you will use only a few hours each season, there is no reason why you should not buy one machine as tenants in common, sharing its cost, maintenance, and use.

Tax Consequences

Because a tenant in common owns his share outright, the tax consequences of tenancy in common are identical with those of sole ownership. The tenant is solely responsible for paying income tax on its yield or sale, and the property becomes part of his estate for both federal and state death tax purposes.

Establishing a Tenancy in Common

By Agreement. When a tenancy in common is set up by agreement among two or more people, the arrangement, no matter how informal, should nevertheless be put into writing in a document that specifies not only the contribution to and the share owned by each tenant but also his responsibilities and his voice in any decisions that will be made about the use, maintenance, or disposition of the property involved.

If the property consists of real estate, the wording of the deed or land contract should clearly indicate a tenancy in common. The same holds true for other kinds of property. Both banks and brokerage firms are quite familiar with tenancy in common, and either the bank signature card or the brokerage account should be marked TEN COM, although even in these cases a written document specifying tenancy in common and the share owned by each tenant will provide the tenants with additional protection. When other kinds of personal property are involved, a bill of sale or a separate document can indicate that a tenancy in common and not a joint tenancy is intended by all parties.

By Court Action. A tenancy in common may also be established by a court of law. In many divorce settlements, especially in community property states (see Chap. 8), the court may order that all property held by the couple in joint tenancy or tenancy by the entirety be converted into a tenancy in common so as to abolish automatic inheritability and to ensure that each tenant has the exclusive right to control and dispose of his or her share.

Court action may also create a tenancy in common when a creditor makes a successful claim against property held in joint tenancy. To satisfy the creditor's claims, a court may order that the debtor's share of the joint tenancy property be turned over to the creditor, who then becomes a tenant in common with the remaining tenant(s).

By Transfer. In some circumstances a tenancy in common may be established by transfer of property owned solely or in joint tenancy. If, for example, one joint tenant sells his share to a third party, the third party becomes a tenant in common with the remaining joint tenant(s). Similarly, the sole owner of a piece of property – income-producing real estate, for example – may sell whatever portion of it he chooses to someone else, who then becomes a tenant in common with the original owner.

By Default. Occasionally a tenancy in common is established by error – through ignorance or as the result of a carelessly drawn deed, land contract, or will. Although, as we have noted, there are situations in which you would like to bequeath something to your survivors as tenants in common, there are many other situations in which you may intend joint tenancy. You may, for example, want to leave your summer cottage to your wife and only son in joint tenancy in order to ensure rights of survivorship. If so, your will should identify the beneficiaries as "Mary Smith and Robert Smith as joint tenants and not as tenants in common." If, instead, your will simply says, "I leave my summer cottage to my wife, Mary Smith, and my son Robert Smith," the probate courts of most states will resolve any ambiguity in favor of tenancy in common.

Similar problems can arise when a bank or brokerage account is established. Particularly in small banks and local branches, bank officers may not be aware of the distinctions among the three forms of co-ownership, and an account intended to be a joint tenancy may be registered erroneously as a tenancy in common if you do not insist on the specific form you prefer.

In general, when most types of property are transferred to two or more persons, the law presumes that a tenancy in common was intended unless the document of transfer clearly specifies joint tenancy or some other form of ownership. The one exception to this presumption involves real estate. In some states, when a deed transferring real estate to husband and wife fails to specify the form of ownership, the presumption is that the spouses intended to own it as tenants by the entirety.

Terminating a Tenancy in Common

If a tenant in common sells his share, the tenancy continues, because the purchaser becomes the new tenant. If, however, all tenants agree to divide the property among themselves (if, for example, it consists of 1,000 bushels of grain), the tenancy ends. The tenancy terminates also if the property is sold by common consent, although the proceeds are regarded as held as a tenancy in common until the money is distributed pro rata among the owners.

COMBINING FORMS OF CO-OWNERSHIP

As we have noted, various forms of ownership can be used for various items of your property. It is equally important to recognize that these forms can often be combined with respect to one item of property.

Suppose, for example, that you have acquired a share of a certificate of deposit as a tenant in common. There is no reason why you cannot transfer this share into joint tenancy with your spouse or a child in order to ensure automatic inheritability. (In a sense, you are already doing this if any corporate stock you own is registered in joint tenancy.)

Given mutual agreement between co-tenants, it is also possible to sell part of a jointly owned asset to someone outside the family. Since automatic inheritability of their respective shares is no longer desired by either the new buyer or the sellers, the property should be transferred to a tenancy in common, but the share retained by the original owners can still be held in joint tenancy between them or, if they are spouses, in tenancy by the entirety.

In sum, there are many combinations and permutations of ownership forms from which you can choose whatever best suits both your personal situation and the nature and value of your assets. If, however, your assets are diverse and your personal situation is subject to change, you are likely to find that the simplest, most efficient, and most flexible form of ownership is not co-ownership but is a revocable trust, which we discuss in the next chapter.

PARTNERSHIP

If you intend to use some of your assets to produce income through a part- or full-time business, you might consider forming a partnership with one or more other people.

A partnership—which is actually a form of tenancy in common— has two principal advantages over being in business for yourself. First, it can make available more money for capitalization of the business than an individual proprietor may be able to muster. Second, and perhaps more important, it can bring to a new enterprise a wider array of abilities and experience than the sole proprietor is likely to have. Restaurants, for example, are often operated by two partners, one of whom is responsible for the food preparation, the other for management of the business. The partners in a small manufacturing firm may be a "Mr. Inside," who is responsible for all aspects of production, and a "Mr. Outside," responsible for sales.

In many circumstances, especially if the business is part-time, small, or just getting under way, forming a partnership is preferable to incorporating (see Chap. 5). To begin with, not only is it less expensive to set up but it also requires far less paperwork, especially in the form of meeting minutes, tax returns, and other reports. Moreover, partnership profits are taxed only once, whereas corporate profits are taxed twice, first as corporate profits, then as dividend income received by the stockholders. Lastly, if a partnership suffers losses, these losses are tax-deductible by the individual partners. Indeed, certain forms of limited partnerships are available to high-income individuals for the express purpose of reducing their income tax.

On the other hand, partnerships have certain inherent disadvantages. Whereas a shareholder in a corporation has limited liability – that is, he can lose no more money than what he invested – the liability of partners is unlimited. Thus, if a partnership suffers a catastrophic loss or incurs some other sort of severe financial obligation, each partner is personally liable and creditors can attach a partner's personal assets that are not invested in the partnership, even though the loss or the liability resulted from the actions of another partner or even an employee.

If, for example, an employee making deliveries in your partnership-owned truck causes damages that exceed the partnership's insurance coverage, the excess would be payable not only by the partnership but also by you personally if the partnership had insufficient assets.

In addition, partnerships, unlike corporations, are not permitted to provide retirement plans, medical plans, life insurance, and other fringe benefits that offer tax advantages both to the firm and to its employees. And, again unlike a corporation, a partnership does not enjoy the 70% exclusion from taxability of dividends paid on stock it owns in domestic corporations (see Chap. 5).

Partnerships, moreover, are less flexible than corporations. A corporate shareholder can usually terminate his involvement with the corporation at any time by transferring his shares – by selling, giving, or bequeathing them to anyone he chooses. A partner, however, usually cannot transfer his status as a partner to anyone without the consent of all the other partners. A partner may, unless prohibited by the partnership agreement, give or sell his *interest* in the partnership to someone else, but such a transfer does not terminate the partnership or entitle the recipient or buyer to participate in the management of the partnership. All that such a transfer involves is the right to a share of the profits and any remaining surplus when the partnership is dissolved.

Establishing a Partnership

A partnership is essentially an association of two or more persons as co-owners to carry on a business for profit. In some situations, one or more of the partners may be a corporation or another partnership.

Unlike a corporate charter, whose form and content must comply strictly with state law, a partnership agreement can be quite informal and may, in fact, be oral. But in view of the potential problems we have referred to above, it is advisable—indeed, essential—that any partnership involving significant investment and other commitments be based on an agreement that has been carefully thought out, put into writing, and signed. Such a partnership agreement usually includes the following:

the name and address of each partner

the name and location of the partnership business

the nature, purpose, scope, and duration of the partnership

the date on which the partnership is to become effective

the cash or other assets contributed by each partner, and whether or not interest is to be paid on invested capital

how profits and losses are to be shared or divided

the powers of each partner (to sign checks, buy materials, etc.), the duties and responsibilities of each, the amount of time each is expected to devote to the business, and any restrictions on the activities of each

the salaries, drawing accounts, and expense accounts to be provided for each partner

how and where the books are to be kept, and how the partnership is to be managed

provisions for the retirement of a partner

provisions for continuing the partnership on the withdrawal or death of a partner: how such a partner's interest will be appraised, whether the remaining partners must buy his interest, and how payment for such interest is to be made

provisions for arbitration of disputes arising between or among the partners

Many states require a new partnership to file with the county clerk a certificate of copartnership (see Figure 4), a form similar to the assumed name certificate required of sole proprietorships doing business under an assumed name (for example, The Booktique). The county clerk has the right to reject a proposed name if it is deemed misleading or if it duplicates or closely resembles the name of an existing entity. The name approved for the partnership is the one that will be used on bank accounts and in all transactions.

Rights and Obligations of Partners

Each partner has the right to use any assets of the partnership in the conduct of partnership business but not for personal, nonbusiness purposes. And each is entitled to his or her stipulated share of the profits. No matter who is responsible for the accounting, the books are open to inspection by any partner at any time.

Certain acts—disposing of the goodwill of the business, for example, or any act that would prevent the firm from carrying on its business—require the unanimous consent of all partners. But unless restricted by the partnership agreement, any partner has the right to sign checks, enter into contracts, and make other commitments on behalf of the partnership. This means, of course, that you must choose as your partners people who are not only solvent, competent, and completely trustworthy but also stable emotionally and maritally. Although your partners do not have your life in their hands, they may have the bulk of your assets there.

A high degree of trustworthiness applies also to the loyalty of individual partners to the partnership. If, for example, you are a full-time partner in a consulting firm and a partnership client approaches you for consultation *as an individual,* the ethics of partnership, as well as the law, normally require that you turn over the consultation fee to the partnership even though you provided the consultation single-handed.

Termination of Partnership

The partners can at any time agree to terminate the partnership and divide its assets among them. The partnership will automatically terminate on the death of one of the partners unless the partnership agreement provides for continuation. When a partner dies, his share of partnership property (motor vehicles, furniture, equipment,

Figure 4
CERTIFICATE OF COPARTNERSHIP

Certificate of Co-Partnership

STATE OF MICHIGAN ⎱
COUNTY OF INGHAM ⎰ SS

FILING FEE, $10.00

THIS CERTIFIES THAT WE, WHOSE NAMES ARE SIGNED HEREUNDER IN FULL, ARE JOINED IN CO-PARTNERSHIP UNDER THE FIRM NAME OF:

NAME OF BUSINESS _____

TYPE OF BUSINESS _____

ADDRESS/LOCATION _____
ADDRESS   CITY   STATE   ZIP

PRINT OR TYPE NAME AND ADDRESSES OF CO PARTNERS

NAME	STREET ADDRESS	CITY OR TOWN

IN WITNESS WHEREOF, WE HAVE THIS DATE _____ 19___, MADE AND SIGNED THIS CERTIFICATE.

THIS CERTIFICATE EXPIRES FIVE (5) YEARS FROM THE DATE OF FILING WITH THE COUNTY CLERK

THIS CERTIFICATE EXPIRES ON _____.

SIGNATURES OF CO PARTNERS

_____   _____

_____   _____

_____   _____

STATE OF MICHIGAN ⎱
COUNTY OF INGHAM ⎰ SS   I, _____

ONE OF THE CO-PARTNERS OF THE SAID FIRM OF _____ (FIRM NAME)
DO HEREBY CERTIFY THAT ALL CO-PARTNERS OF SAID FIRM HAVE HEREIN ABOVE INDIVIDUALLY
SUBSCRIBED THEIR RESPECTIVE NAMES AS WITNESSED BY MYSELF, AND THAT THE PLACE OF
RESIDENCE OF EACH SAID CO-PARTNER AS ABOVE WRITTEN IS TRUE AND CORRECT.

(SIGNED) _____
(ONE OF CO-PARTNERS OF ABOVE NAMED FIRM)

SUBSCRIBED AND SWORN TO BEFORE ME THIS DATE _____ 19_____

_____

NOTARY PUBLIC, _____ COUNTY, MICHIGAN.

MY COMMISSION EXPIRES _____ 19___.

STATE OF MICHIGAN ⎱ SS
COUNTY OF INGHAM ⎰   I, _____
CLERK OF THE COUNTY AFORESAID AND CLERK OF THE CIRCUIT COURT FOR SAID COUNTY, DO
HEREBY CERTIFY THAT I HAVE COMPARED THE WITHIN COPY OF CERTIFICATE SETTING FORTH
THE FULL NAMES OF THE PERSONS OWNING, CONDUCTING OR TRANSACTING BUSINESS UNDER THE
NAME OF _____
TOGETHER WITH THE CERTIFICATE OF FILING ENDORED THEREON, WITH THE ORIGINAL CERTIF-
ICATE HERETOFORE FILED AND NOW REMAINING IN MY OFFICE, AND THAT IT IS A TRUE AND
CORRECT COPY THEREOF, AND OF THE WHOLE OF SUCH ORIGINAL CERTIFICATE AND OF SAID
CERTIFICATE OF FILING.

IN TESTIMONY WHEREOF, I HAVE HEREUNTO SET MY HAND
AND AFFIXED THE SEAL OF SAID CIRCUIT COURT, THIS
DAY OF _____ 19_____
_____
(COUNTY CLERK)
BY _____
(DEPUTY COUNTY CLERK)

leases, real estate, bank funds, accounts receivable) remains with the surviving partners for use in continuing the business, but his *interest* in the partnership—that is, his share of the profits and the actual net worth of the partnership—can, like any other kind of property, be willed to survivors, who may then demand to be bought out by the surviving partners. This is one reason why partnerships often carry substantial insurance coverage on the lives of the partners.

A partnership will terminate when circumstances prevent the continuation of the business—when, for example, one of the partners in a bar or restaurant loses his liquor license. It can also be terminated by a court, in response to a petition by any partner claiming that the partnership cannot earn a profit or that another partner has been judicially declared mentally unsound, continually violates the partnership agreement, or is incapable of performing his partnership duties.

Lastly, unless the partnership agreement provides for continuation of the business, a partnership will terminate when any one of the partners decides to withdraw or is expelled for breaching the partnership agreement. If the remaining partners wish to continue the business, they must form a new partnership. If, however, a partner's voluntary withdrawal constitutes a breach of the partnership agreement, he may be held liable for money damages.

Tax Consequences

As we have noted, a partnership, unlike a corporation, is not treated as an entity separate from the partners with respect to taxes. For income tax purposes, the income and expenses of the partnership are taxed as the income and expenses of the individual partners; that is, all profits (whether they remain in the partnership as working capital or are distributed to the partners as salary or bonuses) "pass through" the partnership and are taxable to the partners individually. The same holds true for any losses that the partnership sustains. They are tax-deductible on the individual partners' tax returns, but each partner can deduce no loss greater than his respective interest in the partnership. Thus, the partnership itself pays no income tax. It merely files with the IRS an informational return that specifies how much each partner has earned or lost.

Protection Against Creditors

Although creditors of the partnership can attach your personal assets if the partnership cannot pay their claims, the reverse is not true.

Your personal creditors cannot attach your interest in the partnership. They can, however, garnish any income you earn from it or any profit it owes you (see Chap. 7).

Is Partnership for You?

As a means of holding assets, the partnership has no advantages over the forms of co-ownership discussed earlier in this chapter. It is useful only if (1) you expect to use your assets in a profit-making enterprise that (2) needs more capital than you can raise as an individual, and/or (3) requires skills or experience that you lack.

For a part-time or small-scale business, the main advantages of partnership—simplicity and informality in getting it under way—can also constitute its principal hazard. "Let's go into partnership!" is a phrase often heard at cocktail parties—an environment that is not conducive to judicious evaluation of either the enterprise or the prospective partners. The fact that the partnership can be launched on the following day may have much to do with the high mortality rate characteristic of this form of ownership. The greater complexity and delay involved in the incorporation of a business provides a useful cooling-off period, and the red tape required by state law and the Internal Revenue Code often protects the prospective incorporators as well as the public.

C H A P T E R 4

LETTING OTHERS OWN IT

If you have relatively few assets and their value is only moderate, and if your family situation seems unlikely to change, one of the forms of co-ownership described in the preceding chapter will probably suit your needs. Joint ownership provides automatic inheritability and can, at least to some extent, protect your assets against creditors' claims and reduce your tax burden. Above all, it usually costs nothing to set up. These advantages may well outweigh its inherent disadvantages.

But if your assets are numerous, diverse, and increasing in value, it can be something of a chore to place each bank account, each stock and bond, each piece of real estate, and each of your other valuable possessions into one or another form of co-ownership. More important, if your future financial needs are unpredictable or if your relationships with family and others are unstable or complex, the inflexibility of joint ownership can sometimes present serious problems. In such circumstances, you are likely to enjoy all the advantages of joint ownership and considerably greater convenience, flexibility, and security if you transfer part or all of your assets into some type of trust.

Because we have all encountered, in novels and movies, characters who live in luxurious idleness, supported by "a trust my grandfather set up for me," many of us think of a trust as an instrument that the very rich use to avoid taxes or to exercise fiscal control over their playboy, spendthrift, or black-sheep children. Trusts, many middle-income people assume, are for the Rockefellers and Vanderbilts, not for themselves.

In reality, trusts of one kind or another are becoming increasingly common among people whose net worth is far below the millionaire level. As tax burdens rise, as people accumulate more assets and hence become more concerned with estate planning and probate avoidance, as family stability diminishes and remarriage and cohabitation become more common, and as more lawyers become familiar with and recommend trusts, the old stereotypes are disappearing. Instead, there is increasing recognition of a trust's many advantages and a growing realization that a trust is neither difficult nor expensive to set up. In fact, as we shall see shortly, you may already have some property that is now in a trust, even though you may not be aware of it.

TRUSTS—THE BASIC CONCEPT

When you establish a trust, you turn over the ownership and management of your property to a trustee. This may strike you as a disconcerting and risky idea but, although the trustee "owns" the property, you need not relinquish ultimate control over your property or over the actions of the trustee. (In fact, you may, if you wish, serve as the trustee or co-trustee of your own trust.) The basic reason for the transfer of ownership to the trustee is that it changes your legal relationship to the property, and this change offers you some important advantages that are not available under joint ownership.

There are several types of trust, each with distinctive features that serve specific purposes. But despite the variations, a general definition is possible: A trust is a legal entity (similar in some respects to a corporation) that is permitted to own, manage, reinvest, and ultimately distribute any kind of property. The property it manages is transferred into the trust by one or more *grantors* (sometimes called settlors or trustors), and the trust is administered by one or more *trustees* for the current or future benefit of one or more *beneficiaries*.

The most widely used form of trust—the living, or *inter vivos*, revocable trust—has four very significant characteristics. First, and most important, in this form of trust *any or all of the three roles—grantor, trustee, or beneficiary—may be filled by the same person or persons.* Moreover, the grantor may at any time replace the current trustees or beneficiaries with new ones. Thus, if you establish a revocable trust, as grantor you can, if you wish, serve as your own trustee or you can designate, either as trustee or as co-trustee, a relative, a friend, a lawyer, a bank, or a trust company. If you prefer, you can serve as trustee during your lifetime and designate one or more successor trustees to take over administration of the trust when you no longer want to serve, if you become incapacitated, or when you die. The same flexibility applies to your designation of beneficiaries. You may, for example, designate yourself and/or your spouse as beneficiaries during your lifetime, and your children or any other person or institution as beneficiaries after your death. And you can change beneficiaries whenever you like, prior to your incapacity or death.

In a revocable trust, whether or not you serve as a trustee, you are, as a grantor, fully entitled to move property into and out of the trust or to sell or gift off trust property at any time and to use whatever income the trust-held property earns. In short, you can retain full control over trust assets as well as the actions of the trustee, even though in a strictly legal sense the assets are titled in the trustee's name, not in yours.

The second significant characteristic of a revocable trust is that *the assets held in trust are not part of your probate estate*. On your death, they can pass to the beneficiaries you designate in the trust document just as swiftly as they would if held in joint ownership.

Third, *a trust can serve as your own (and perhaps sole) beneficiary.* That is, upon your death, your will can bequeath everything you possess to the trust. This tactic does not avoid probate but, as we shall see, it assures you far more control over your property after your death than you can enjoy through joint ownership or through a will that bequeaths your assets directly and unconditionally to your beneficiaries.

Lastly, *a trust can outlive the grantor by many decades*, since any trustee can be succeeded by another. This longevity extends your control over your property far beyond your death, since whatever you place in a trust can be passed on not only to your immediate beneficiaries but also to future generations under conditions that you can now specify in the trust document.

THE ADVANTAGES OF TRUSTS

Trusts are proliferating because they provide all the advantages of joint ownership—and more. Since not all types of trust offer the same advantages, the discussion that follows does not apply to all of them. But because some advantages will appeal to you more than others, a thoughtful reading may help you identify the type of trust that best suits your purposes, your assets, and the needs of your survivors.

Convenience plus Management

A trust can offer you even more convenience than joint ownership. If you are hospitalized or traveling, or otherwise unavailable or incapacitated, the trustee (or your co-trustee or successor trustee if you are serving as your own trustee) can manage your assets for you. After your death, the trustee or successor trustee can continue managing the trust assets for as long as you specify in the trust document, making partial distributions to your beneficiaries according to your instructions, investing and reinvesting, and ultimately making final distribution.

In addition to convenience, a trust offers the grantors an opportunity for continuous professional management of their assets. If, for example, your assets include a securities portfolio, and if you are unsophisticated about the stock market or simply unwilling to devote time and attention to monitoring your securities, designating a bank or trust company as the trustee may give you a far higher yield than you could achieve by yourself. Professional trustees may be of value, also, if your property includes income-producing real estate, which you can't or don't want to manage personally. The fees charged by some professional trustees, however, are not inconsiderable and may well cancel out any gains achieved through professional management.

Flexibility during Life

If either your future financial needs or the stability of your marriage relationship is unpredictable, a trust can give you far more flexibility and control than joint ownership. As we have seen, joint ownership can be very difficult to revoke, and anything you place in joint ownership may pass, at least to some extent, out of your exclusive control. If, for example, you transfer most of your assets into joint ownership with your spouse, you may not be able to use them for a new business venture without your spouse's consent. Should you divorce, your spouse will receive half of the jointly held assets whether or not he or she helped you acquire them. Moreover, if you remarry, any assets you place in joint ownership with your second spouse cannot be given or bequeathed to the children of your first marriage without your new spouse's consent.

If, on the other hand, you place your assets in a trust, you retain full control over them and can use them for any purpose at any time prior to your incapacity or death. You can provide for automatic inheritance by your spouse by naming him/her as the trust's beneficiary, but you can easily change beneficiaries at any time if your marital situation should change, and you can make provisions for children by a prior marriage or for anyone else you choose. In some states, in fact, a trust can be used to disinherit a spouse—an action that cannot be accomplished through use of a will.

A trust, then, can remain revocable during your lifetime and still achive prompt inheritance without probate administration. In addition to avoiding probate, a trust can serve most of the purposes of a will. Like joint ownership, however, it does not relieve you of the need to make a will (see Chap. 3).

Control after Death

If you bequeath your property outright to beneficiaries by means of a will, you will have no control over it after your death. Under state law, the probate court will require your personal representative to liquidate your estate as expeditiously as possible and to distribute the proceeds to your beneficiaries, regardless of whether prompt liquidation is advisable or whether your beneficiaries are able and willing to use the proceeds judiciously.

Thus, for example, if you own a promising business, it will almost certainly have to be sold promptly on your death, even though it might triple in value if it were permitted to operate for another two or three years. But if, instead, you transfer your business to a trust and designate a competent trustee, there is no reason why your business could not continue to operate indefinitely after you die or at least until it reached its full potential value.

In addition to protecting your assets from premature liquidation, a trust can be far more effective than joint ownership in protecting them from dissipation by your surviving beneficiaries. When one joint owner dies, the fate of jointly held property depends on the financial acuity of the survivor. If, for example, the surviving joint owner is an elderly widow, she may be susceptible to all sorts of investment schemes or confidence games. Or if the survivor is an immature or unstable child, his or her inheritance may be dissipated in other ways. If, on the other hand, the property is held in a trust managed by a competent trustee, you, as grantor, can set the conditions and the timetable under which the inheritance will be passed on to your beneficiaries, and you can enjoy greater confidence that its value is likely to be preserved or increased.

This assurance of stability and continuity becomes even more important if you have a disabled child or some other dependent who is likely to require lifetime care. In such circumstances a trust can protect the beneficiary's financial interests even though a guardian may have to be appointed to make custodial decisions and take care of the ward's other personal needs.

For example, if you have nominated your sister as the guardian of your minor or disabled son, your sister will, on your death, assume custody of the child and responsibility for meeting his day-to-day needs. But if your sister has no ability or desire to manage money or other assets, the child's inheritance could be placed in a trust with a local bank named as trustee to manage the assets and make periodic distributions to the child's guardian.

In order to ensure that the trustee bank manages the inheritance competently, remains responsive to the child's needs, and does not charge unreasonable annual fees, your trust can specifically grant to the guardian (your sister) the power to discharge the trustee bank and to appoint as successor trustee "any bank or trust company in the U.S.A. which is authorized by law to administer trusts."

Protection against Creditors' Claims

All types of trusts provide protection against creditors' claims after the death of the grantors. Some types offer such protection during the grantor's lifetime as well, but, as we shall see, this protection comes at a very high price.

Tax Consequences

Some types of trust offer the possibility of reducing or totally avoiding income tax, federal estate tax, or both. An irrevocable trust, for example, allows you to shift income tax liability for the yield on its assets from yourself to beneficiaries who are in a lower tax bracket. But most such trusts require you to relinquish—at least temporarily and more often permanently—any control over the assets and any benefit from their yield. Except on a small scale (see p. 80), they offer advantages only to those who are rich enough to dispense completely and irrevocably with a part of their assets.

A generation-skipping trust, which may be revocable or irrevocable, and which may be established during your lifetime or by your will after your death, can avoid double liability for federal estate tax. If, for example, you willed some assets to a child of yours and he, in turn, willed all or part of them to his child, the assets could be subject to federal estate tax twice, first as part of your estate and later as part of your child's estate. If, however, you set up a generation-skipping trust with a grandchild as beneficiary, your child may receive the trust income and your grandchild may eventually inherit the assets, but federal estate tax will be payable only once—by your estate upon your death.

THE REVOCABLE LIVING TRUST

Trusts can be classified in many ways, but for our purposes the most useful approach is to distinguish between *revocable* and *irrevocable* living trusts. Although the revocable trust lacks some of the advantages offered by the irrevocable trust, it is far more widely used—and for good reasons. We shall deal first, therefore, with the revocable living trust and then, more briefly, with the irrevocable version.

The most important feature of a revocable living trust is implied by its name: You, as grantor, can freely transfer property into and out of the trust, change your designation of the trustees and beneficiaries, alter or modify the conditions under which the beneficiaries are entitled to receive their benefits, or even terminate the trust altogether at any time before you become mentally incompetent or die. This revocability offers you complete freedom and control; it permits you to appoint a trustee, monitor his performance, and replace him as often as necessary until you find someone thoroughly competent to manage the trust after your incompetency or death.

The principal reason for establishing a revocable living trust is the avoidance of probate. If you become incompetent, the trustee manages your assets without the expense, frustrations, and indignity of probate court guardianship proceedings. On your death, none of the property held in the trust is probatable, because it is titled in the trustee's name, not in yours. Thus, by transferring all your property into such a trust, you avoid not only the inevitable costs, delays, and frustrations of probate but also the attendant publicity. Probate is a public procedure; through probate records, anyone interested can find out the nature and value of your estate and identify the beneficiaries of your will, but the after-death transfer of assets from a trust to its beneficiaries is completely private.

Many people believe that by setting up a revocable living trust they can reduce or avoid income, estate, or gift taxes. This is not true. Because the trust is revocable and the grantor has full use of trust-owned property, the grantor remains fully responsible for income tax on the property's earnings, and the full value of the trust's assets is included as part of his estate for estate-tax purposes. When a grantor transfers property into a revocable living trust, no gift tax is involved because no gift is considered completed until after his death, when the property is managed for and distributed to the trust-designated beneficiaries.

The Totten Trust

An easy way to familiarize yourself with the basic principles of a revocable living trust is to try out, on a small scale and at no cost, a somewhat limited version known as a *Totten trust, bank account trust, or discretionary revocable trust account.* This type of trust is recognized by most states and is quite likely to be available at your local bank. Setting it up involves nothing more than filling out a special signature card designating yourself as trustee and your spouse, child, or anyone else you choose as the account's beneficiary (see Figure 5).

Like any other bank account, a Totten trust account is used for cash deposits, but it differs from a conventional bank account in three respects: (1) it provides for the designation of one or more trustees and one or more beneficiaries; (2) upon your death, the balance of the account passes automatically to the account-designated beneficiary without probate administration; and (3) funds in the account are usable by you at any time but they cannot be withdrawn by your beneficiary or attached by his creditors during your lifetime or reached by your creditors after your death.

If you have read the preceding chapter, you may wonder why a Totten trust is preferable to joint ownership, since both types of ownership avoid probate by providing for automatic inheritance. There are two reasons. First, once joint ownership is established it may well be irreversible, whereas the Totten trust permits you not

Figure 5
BANK ACCOUNT CARD: TOTTEN TRUST ACCOUNT

DISCRETIONARY REVOCABLE TRUST ACCOUNT

Date_____   Account No._____

(1)_____As Trustee ⎫ Or the
                        Social Security Number   ⎬ Survivor
and (2)_____As Trustee ⎭ Thereof
                        Social Security Number

For_____Beneficiary ⎫ Or the
                                                                  ⎬ Survivor
and_____Beneficiary ⎭ Thereof
Type (Last Name)   (First Name)   (Middle Name)

As trustees with right of survivorship, the undersigned hereby apply for membership in the

CAPITOL SAVINGS & LOAN ASSOCIATION
112 E. Allegan St.   Lansing, Michigan

and for issuance of _____ Account thereof in their names as trustees de-
scribed as aforesaid, subject to the Laws of the State of Michigan, the rules and regulations of the
Savings and Loan supervisory authority of the State of Michigan and the Articles of Incorporation and
By-Laws of the Association, as they now are or as they may hereafter be amended. You are directed
to act pursuant to writing bearing the signature of any one of said trustees, shown below, in all matters
related to this account. It is agreed by the signatory parties with each other and by the parties with
you that any funds placed in or added to the account by any one of the parties whether in his trustee
or individual capacity is and shall be conclusively intended to be a gift and delivery at that time of
such funds to the trust estate.
If there is only one trustee, beneficiary or grantor then the plural form of designation shall be
considered singular in the application and trust agreement.

Signature_____As Trustee
                                        Address
Signature_____As Trustee
                                        Address
As Trustees for_____

Address_____ Beneficiaries of the Survivors
or survivor thereof as specified in trust agreement on reverse side hereof.
Revocable Joint or Individual Trust Account for 1 or more Beneficiaries.

(front side)

DISCRETIONARY REVOCABLE TRUST AGREEMENT

Trust Agreement Regarding Account No._____

The funds in the account indicated on the reverse side of this instrument, together with earnings
thereon, and any future additions thereto are conveyed to the trustees (who are also grantors herein)
for the beneficiaries or the survivor as indicated. The conditions of said trust are: (1) The trustees are
authorized to hold, manage, invest and reinvest said funds in their sole discretion: (2) The undersigned
grantors of the survivor thereof reserve the right to revoke said trust in part or in full at any time and
any partial or complete withdrawal by the trustees, or survivor thereof, if they are the grantors shall be
a revocation to the extent of such withdrawal, but no other revocation shall be valid unless written
notice by said trustees, grantors or survivor thereof is given to the Institution named on the reverse
side of this card: (3) This trust, subject to the right of revocation shall terminate upon the death of all
the grantors or upon the death of all said beneficiaries prior thereto. If at the death of all grantors any
of said beneficiaries are surviving the proceeds shall be delivered to said surviving beneficiaries; if all
the beneficiaries die prior to all the grantors then said trust forthwith terminates and becomes the
property of the grantors or the survivor thereof; (4) The Institution in which such funds are invested
is authorized to pay the same or to act in any respect affecting said account before or after the
termination of this trust upon the signature of anyone of the trustees or the survivor thereof and has
no responsibility to follow the application of the funds.

This_____day of _____19_____

_____Grantor_____Grantor

(back side)

only to use the money at any time and for any purpose during your lifetime but also to change beneficiaries at will. Second, some forms of joint ownership permit either tenant (even the noncontributor) to withdraw and use all the jointly held funds, whereas the beneficiary you designate in a Totten trust cannot withdraw any of the funds until your death. Both of these differences give you a degree of control that is simply not available with joint ownership.

Although the Totten trust is restricted to savings accounts offered by banks, it illustrates the considerable flexibility provided by the typical revocable living trust. You have full use of the money during your lifetime. Moreover, when death seems imminent you can liquidate most of your property, deposit the proceeds in a Totten trust, and thus avoid probate of the entire balance.

The Totten trust has, however, a number of limitations. Because it is restricted to cash deposits, it provides no opportunity for increasing the yield at a higher rate than the usually conservative rates offered by banks. And, although you can designate an account beneficiary, you cannot specify either the age that the beneficiary must reach or the conditions he or she must meet in order to claim the inheritance. Unlike a formal revocable living trust, which can outlive you, the Totten trust terminates automatically on your death, at which time the account balance passes immediately to the designated beneficiary or to the beneficiary's guardian if the beneficiary is a minor. And, like all revocable living trusts, the Totten trust offers you no tax advantages whatever.

Despite its limitations, the Totten trust can offer you some experience with a revocable living trust. If you don't like it, you can always close it out with no loss or you can maintain it with a minimum balance so that it stands ready for use if your financial situation or your life expectancy changes. If it does seem clearly useful, you can either continue to use it actively or you can realize the same advantages with far more flexibility by creating a more formal revocable living trust.

The Formal Revocable Living Trust

Setting up a living revocable trust is a serious but not necessarily expensive undertaking. It requires that you think carefully about your choice of a trustee because an unsuitable trustee, even though you can replace him before you die, can do considerable damage before you discover it. A revocable living trust also requires a comprehensive and carefully worded trust document, which should be prepared by a lawyer experienced in estate planning. But before spending your own time on thinking about the choice of a trustee and your lawyer's time on formulating the trust document, you need to make some clear decisions about what you expect a trust to accomplish for you.

What probably motivates most people to set up a revocable living trust is the desire to avoid probate of their estates. Although joint ownership also avoids probate, a trust offers greater protection in some respects. Like joint ownership, it may protect your property against creditors' claims after your death; in addition, it is less vulnerable to lawsuits brought by disinherited heirs in an attempt to contest your will or to challenge the automatic inheritance of your jointly owned property. Indeed, a trust can be used to disinherit most of your lawful heirs—in some states, even a spouse.

The probate avoidance feature of trusts is especially valuable if your assets include a business of some sort. If you bequeath your business through a will, it may have to come to a halt while your estate is being probated; the probate court may even require its immediate liquidation. If your business is transferred through use of a trust, however, it can continue without interruption, except for any administrative or operational problems created by your own death.

Placing your business in a revocable living trust is especially useful if you are uncertain about a successor to your business. If, for example, your daughter seems the logical successor but you have some doubts about her ability, placing the business in a trust while you are alive and letting her manage it as the trustee or co-trustee can give you an opportunity to observe her ability and motivation but leave you, as grantor, free to terminate her trusteeship if she fails to meet your expectations.

If, on the other hand, no ongoing business is involved and you simply want to avoid probate administration of your assets, you may serve as your own trustee (or as co-trustee with your spouse or an adult child) and designate as successor trustee the same kind of person you would choose as a personal representative if you merely used a will: your spouse, a trusted younger relative or friend, or perhaps a bank or trust company if your estate is large or complex. On your death, the successor trustee will see that all trust assets are properly managed until they are distributed to the beneficiaries according to the terms of the trust, after which the trust will then terminate.

But a trust can do much more than eliminate the problems of

probate. Its ability to survive your death can give you control over your assets long after death. If you pass property on to your beneficiaries outright by will or through joint ownership, and if you die prematurely, your property will pass immediately to your beneficiaries even though your spouse may be unable to manage it or your children, though legally adults, may not be mature enough to protect it and use it productively. If, instead, you pass your property on by use of a trust, you can not only protect your assets against misuse or dissipation but you can also extend for many years the protection of a spouse, a child, or anyone else who may not be competent to manage them. If this is your purpose, the trustee(s) or successor trustee(s) you choose should have not only the skills needed to manage your assets but also the ability to deal humanely and sensitively with the needs of your beneficiaries or their guardians.

In addition to protecting your assets after your death, a trust can, during your lifetime, relieve you of the responsibility of managing your property, whether it consists of real estate, personal property, or both. If you choose a bank or trust company as trustee, you can empower the trustee to manage all your assets, to sell or trade them on a discretionary basis, and to send you an income check each month or at other regular intervals.

This, of course, entails some risk, because some institutional trustees, including those who serve as trustees for huge pension funds, have in recent years shown poor investment judgment. But if you set up a revocable living trust of this kind and monitor it carefully, you have the opportunity to evaluate the trustee's performance and to make a change if you are not satisfied. We shall deal in detail with the choice of trustee later in this chapter, because your choice will depend in large part on the type of revocable living trust you choose.

Choosing a Type of Trust

Having noted the various functions that a revocable living trust can perform, you can now choose the type of trust that best suits your purposes. To begin with, you need to decide whether your trust should be *funded* or *unfunded*.

A funded trust, as the name implies, is one that owns and manages the grantor's property immediately on its establishment. No revocable trust can be used to avoid probate unless or until it is funded with your assets, because only property that belongs to the trust is removed from the grantor's probate estate.

Unfunded trusts are empty or "dry" at the time of their creation; they are set up in anticipation of future transfers. Although some-states prohibit the establishment of unfunded trusts, this restriction can be easily circumvented by creating the trust with a token amount of perhaps $10. Unfunded trusts do nothing to avoid probate, but they offer certain other advantages. Each of the types discussed below is intended to serve a specific purpose.

A *standby trust* is one that can go into action when the grantor is unavailable (if he is traveling abroad, for example) or becomes incapacitated or incompetent. The trustee, who of course should not be the grantor, simply manages property that the grantor transfers into the trust when circumstances require it.

A *revocable life insurance trust* serves as the beneficiary of the grantor's life insurance policies. It is unfunded until, on the grantor's death, it receives the proceeds of his policies, which it then manages and distributes to the beneficiaries he has named in the trust document according to the conditions he has specified.

There are several reasons why it may be more sensible to name such a trust rather than your individual survivors as the beneficiary of your life insurance proceeds. If, for example, your spouse is unso-phisticated in handling money, trust management can prevent your life insurance proceeds from being squandered, thus depriving your children of benefits intended for them. Or if your children, who may be either primary or contingent beneficiaries, seem unlikely to spend the proceeds in ways of which you approve, the trustee can exercise total control. Perhaps more important, a trustee who is chosen judiciously and given sufficient discretion by the trust document can deal fairly and sensibly with situations that arise after your death: the incapacity or premature death of one or more of your beneficiaries, the birth of a disabled grandchild, or some other unforeseeable events.

Unlike an irrevocable life insurance trust, discussed in the last section of this chapter, the revocable life insurance trust offers no advantages with respect to income tax or federal estate tax. It may, however, depending on your state's laws, protect your life insurance proceeds from claims of creditors and it will protect the proceeds from the delays and costs of probate administration—problems that are unavoidable if you name your estate or your personal representative as the beneficiary of your life insurance policies.

An unfunded *trust*, accompanied by a "pour-over" will, serves essentially the same purpose as a life insurance trust except that its function is broader: It becomes the beneficiary not only of your life insurance proceeds but also of part or all of your estate, which is "poured over" by your will to the trustee. Like the life insurance trust, it helps to protect and enhance your assets, but it also provides privacy during the probate process. When a will is probated, your estate becomes a public record for all to see. Hence, if your will specifies individual bequests, anyone interested can find out whom you disinherited as well as who your beneficiaries are, what share of your assets each received, and their respective values. But if the sole beneficiary of your will is the trustee of a trust, and if only the trust document spells out what you are leaving to each beneficiary, curious outsiders can learn only the total amount of your estate and not its ultimate distribution to the individual beneficiaries.

Although each of the unfunded trusts we have described may be useful, you should bear in mind that none of them except the life insurance trust can be used to avoid probate, because they become funded only through your will. Moreover, such trusts, because they become operative only after your death, offer you no opportunity to monitor the performance of the trustee. On the other hand, there is no reason why a *funded* trust, which does avoid probate, cannot be used for each of the purposes served by unfunded trusts.

One reason for establishing an unfunded rather than a funded trust is that you will pay no trustee fees as long as the trust remains empty. Some people set up an unfunded trust in anticipation of assets they do not yet have or as a future recipient of assets they prefer to retain in other forms of ownership for the time being. Furthermore, as we have noted, an unfunded living trust accompanied by a "pour-over" will established before death provides survivors with more privacy than a testamentary (will-created) trust.

Choosing a Trustee

As should be apparent by now, the choice of a trustee depends heavily on the purposes for which you are creating the trust. If you have hitherto managed your assets competently, and if your purpose is simply to avoid probate and to pass your property on to your beneficiaries immediately after your death, you may appoint yourself as trustee and designate as successor trustee your spouse, an adult child, a sibling or other relative, or a close (and preferably younger) friend. In such circumstances the trust is likely to be short-lived and the assets are unlikely to require professional management. Bear in mind, however, that the successor trustee may take over long before you die—for example, should you become disabled or incompetent.

If, on the other hand, you want the trust to continue for some time after your death in order to protect and gradually distribute the assets to one or more of your beneficiaries, your choice of trustee becomes somewhat more difficult. On the one hand, a bank or a trust company offers you the advantages of continuity, management experience, and careful attention to your investment. But such institutional trustees, aside from costing the trust more in the way of fees, may very well fail or refuse to deal with your beneficiaries' needs or changing circumstances with the warmth and understanding that a relative or a close friend of yours could be expected to show. On the other hand, a relative or a friend who is highly empathetic may have disastrously poor financial judgment.

Some grantors resolve this dilemma by appointing as co-trustees a bank for financial management and a friend or relative to recognize and satisfy the beneficiaries' personal needs. Even if the trust document is very carefully drawn, however, this arrangement may produce conflict and possible impasse between the co-trustees. In fact, banks and other institutional trustees, in anticipation of such time-consuming conflicts, may charge higher fees when a co-trustee is involved.

Institutional trustees may not be ideally suitable for a trust with assets of less than $50,000–$100,000. Because some state laws generally limit trustees' annual fees to a percentage of the value of the trust assets or of the income produced by these assets, many institutional trustees consider trusts of moderate value to be more trouble than they're worth and hence do not devote much time or care to their management. Large urban banks rarely accept trusts whose asset value is less than $300,000. And even when motivated by the high fees to be earned from very large trusts, some professional managers perform poorly in terms of investing trust assets.

Generally speaking, your primary concern in choosing an individual as a trustee should center on his or her integrity, experience, judgment in managing the assets, and understanding and flexibility in dealing with the beneficiaries. You should also be concerned with trustee life expectancy and reject a person whom the trust seems likely to outlive. Since no trustee is likely to meet every one of these criteria, some compromise is almost inevitable. In addition, it is essential to name one or more successor trustees because of the possibility that the trustee you have named may die, or become unable to accept the trusteeship, or resign after accepting it.

In choosing an institutional trustee, the length, breadth, and quality of its trust experience are important considerations. How long has its trust department been in existence? Does the trust department consist of a single young trust officer or does it have several officers backed by a team of managers skilled in investments? Most important, what rate of income and growth has it achieved recently in managing its trust portfolio?

Establishing a Trust

The basis of every trust is a document that defines the terms of the trust in much the same way as a charter and bylaws govern the activities of a corporation. The trust document spells out quite explicitly what the trustee(s) may and may not do, how long the trust is to exist, whether it is revocable or irrevocable, who the beneficiaries are, when and how they are to receive the trust income and assets, and what conditions they must meet in order to receive them. If you bear in mind that any beneficiary can at any time file a lawsuit charging the trustee with violating the terms of the trust, or breaching his fiduciary responsibilities, you can readily see that the trust document must be drafted with great care if it is to carry out your wishes precisely and effectively.

Figure 6, an example of a basic revocable living trust, illustrates the general style and content of a trust document. You should not use it as a model for a trust of your own, because every trust document must reflect not only the basic purposes of the trust but also the exact intentions of the individual grantor and, in some instances, the special circumstances of each beneficiary as well as the special nature of any of the assets. It is almost impossible for a pre-printed form to do this accurately and precisely. Moreover, a trust document must be carefully coordinated with your will, with any property held in joint ownership, and with all your other estate planning strategies, in order to avoid contradictions and inconsistences.

In recent years, a number of books have been published that offer do-it-yourself instructions for preparing a trust document. In addition, a number of telemarketing firms have exploited the public (mainly the elderly) by offering trust preparation to people who have no need for it. At best, such firms overcharge their clients; at worst,

Figure 6
REVOCABLE LIVING TRUST

DECLARATION OF TRUST made May 8, 1995, by JOHN DOE, MARY DOE, WILLIAM DOE, and JANE HARRIS, hereinafter called "Trustees", with reference to the following facts:

(a) John and Mary are husband and wife and hold title to all of their property as joint tenants or tenants by the entireties;

(b) William Doe and Jane Harris are their only children; each of them has children;

(c) John and Mary would like to avoid probate, not only in the event of the death or disability of one of them, but also on the death of the survivor of them, but want assurance that, in the event of the disability of one or both of them, property will be applied toward his, her or their care and, upon the death of the survivor of them, will be distributed to their issue who survive such survivor, per stirpes;

(d) The parties have decided upon holding such property in joint tenancy, with full rights of survivorship, and without any mention of a trust on the record, but with a declaration and acknowledgment that those who succeed, or the one who succeeds, to the title on the death or disability of another or others are, or is, actually holding as trustees, or trustee, for the purposes and on the conditions hereinafter set forth.

THE PARTIES AGREE:

1. ESTABLISHMENT OF TRUST. Any property assigned, heretofore or hereafter, by John and/or Mary to the Trustees, as joint tenants or otherwise, shall be deemed trust property and Trustees agree to hold the same in trust for the purposes and on the conditions hereinafter set forth.

2. RESERVATIONS. John and Mary (or the survivor of them) reserve(s) the right to amend or revoke this trust and Trustees agree to reassign or reconvey to them or the survivor of them any property affected by the exercise of such right.

3. TRUSTEE. If one acting as a trustee shall become disabled as defined in the paragraph entitled "DISABILITY" in Article V, he shall be deemed to have resigned.

If none of the parties is acting as a trustee, the personal representative of the last to act or, if he has none appointed within thirty (30) days after he ceases to act, EAST LANSING STATE BANK shall become trustee by filing with a beneficiary hereunder a written acceptance of trust.

Individual trustees shall be reimbursed for their reasonable out-of-pocket expenses, but shall receive no additional compensation for their services. A corporate trustee shall be entitled to reimbursement for expenses and fees in accordance with its published fee schedule in effect at the time the services for which the fee is charged are performed, and if there is no such fee schedule then in effect, such fees as, from time to time, are recognized in the area as ordinary and reasonable for the services it performs.

Figure 6 (continued)
REVOCABLE LIVING TRUST

4. DISTRIBUTION.

DURING THE LIVES OF JOHN AND MARY

INCOME: While both John and Mary are living and not disabled, all of the net income shall be paid to them or at their direction. If both of them become disabled, Trustees shall, in their discretion, apply income for their benefit or accumulate income and thereafter treat it as corpus. After the death of John or Mary, Trustees shall likewise pay or apply net income to or for the benefit of the survivor of them.

CORPUS: Trustees may pay to either John or Mary from the corpus of the trust from time to time, such further accounts (even to the exhaustion of the trust) as in their discretion they deem necessary or advisable to properly maintain him or her in the style to which he or she is presently accustomed, and shall do so if he or she becomes disabled; such payments may include amounts to or for the benefit of persons dependent upon them for support and premiums on life insurance on either of them or such persons whether or not such policies are payable to this trust.

ON DEATH: Upon the death of John or Mary, Trustees shall pay the expenses of his or her last illness and burial and all debts and taxes and other charges against him or her or arising because of his or her death which shall seem proper; upon the death of the survivor of them, Trustees shall pay such expenses, debts, taxes and charges arising because of the survivor's death and shall pay over all remaining property, both corpus and accumulated income, to the issue of John and Mary surviving such survivor, per stirpes, their children to be the stock.

Notwithstanding the foregoing, if any distributee has not attained his majority, his share shall be continued in trust, with Trustees accumulating income and distributing to him so much thereof and of corpus from time to time as they deem for his best interests and welfare and upon his reaching his majority, paying over to him property, if any, remaining; and, in the event of his death, paying property on hand to his personal representative.

5. MISCELLANEOUS.

SURVIVAL DEFINED. No person shall be considered to have survived another if he shall die within thirty (30) days after the death of the other.

DISABILITY. If two medical doctors determine that a beneficiary or a trustee is suffering from physical or mental disability to the extent he is incapable of exercising judgment about or attending to financial and property transactions, such determination reduced to writing and delivered to any beneficiary or contingent beneficiary under this agreement, or to another trustee, shall be conclusive for the purposes of this agreement.

6. ADMINISTRATIVE POWERS. Trustees shall have the power to retain, sell, invest and reinvest, loan, improve, lease and borrow.

Figure 6 (continued)
REVOCABLE LIVING TRUST

7. ACCOUNTING. So long as Mary lives and is not disabled, Trustees need keep no accounts because of the control which she has retained. However, in the event of the disability or death of Mary, Trustees shall keep an account of receipts and disbursements and of property on hand at the end of the accounting period and shall deliver copies to the beneficiaries or, if one is a minor, to one with whom he makes his home.

8. EXCULPATORY. No purchaser from or other person dealing with Trustees shall be responsible for the application of any purchase money or other thing of value paid or delivered to them, but the receipt of Trustees shall be a full discharge; and no purchaser or other person dealing with Trustees and no issuer, or transfer agent or other agent of any issuer of any securities to which any dealing with Trustees should relate, shall be under any obligation to ascertain or inquire into the power of Trustees to purchase, sell, exchange, transfer, mortgage, pledge, lease, distribute or otherwise in any manner dispose of or deal with any security or any other property held by Trustees or comprised in this estate.

The certificate of the Trustees that they are acting according to the terms of this instrument shall fully protect all persons dealing with the Trustees.

9. CONFLICT OF LAWS. All questions concerning the validity, construction and administration of the trust shall be determined under the laws of the State of Michigan.

IN WITNESS WHEREOF, the parties have executed this instrument.

Witness:

Lawrence L. Black	John Doe
Belinda B. Blue	Mary Doe
	William Doe
	Jane Harris

STATE OF MICHIGAN)
)ss
COUNTY OF INGHAM)

On this 8th day of May, 1995, before me, a Notary Public, in and for said County, personally appeared John Doe, Mary Doe, William Doe, and Jane Harris, to me known to be the same persons described in and who executed the within instrument, who acknowledged the same to be their free act and deed.

INSTRUMENT PREPARED BY:
Lawrence L. Black
Attorney at Law
101 Main Street
Lansing, Michigan 48933

Belinda B. Blue, Notary Public
Ingham County, Michigan
My Commission Expires: 1/8/98
Lansing, Michigan 48933

they persuade the clients to move their assets into dubious investments on which the firms earn commissions. Both the books and the telemarketers offer a one-size-fits-all trust document that consists almost entirely of "boilerplate." For these reasons, you should not rely on these sources for preparation of a trust document.

Your choice of a lawyer may be almost as crucial to the success of your trust as your choice of trustee. Above all, the lawyer you choose should be experienced in estate planning. If your regular lawyer has no such experience but you think that asking him for a referral may hurt his feelings, you can probably find one through the referral service of your local bar association, through the clerk of your county probate court, or by a call to your bank's trust department.

Some estate lawyers charge their clients on an hourly basis, the fees ranging from perhaps $75 per hour for young lawyers in rural areas to well over $200 for high-prestige urban firms. Others charge a set fee for preparing and funding a trust, the amount ranging from $1,000 to $2,000. Drafting a trust should not involve more than five or six hours of a lawyer's time, and this money is likely to be well spent if it protects you against the deficiencies of do-it-yourself books and ready-made forms.

Although any lawyer experienced in estate planning is likely to draft a satisfactory trust document, the checklist shown in Table 5 should guide you in your preliminary discussion with your lawyer and should help you to make sure that the document he produces reflects your intentions and meets all your needs.

THE INTEREST-FREE LOAN

So far we have discussed trust arrangements that, because they are revocable, offer you no relief from income tax or from federal gift and estate taxes on trust-held assets. If a reduction of income tax is your principal aim, you might consider one alternative that sacrifices some degree of revocability but offers in return some measure of tax relief: the interest-free loan.

If you have a money market account currently yielding $2,500 a year in interest, you must pay income tax—at your highest bracket—on this yield. If, however, you lend the money to a child, a widowed mother, or some other relative, the money is no longer yours but

Table 5
ELEMENTS OF A TRUST AGREEMENT

What a trust MUST include	*What a trust MAY include*
Name of grantor	
Name of trustee and successor trustee	Selection of individual or corporate trustee; standby provision for trustee to take over when grantor is ill, absent or dead
Name of beneficiaries and alternate beneficiaries	Selection of individual or charitable beneficiaries; authority of beneficiary to replace trustee
Purposes of trust	
Duration of trust	
Whether trust is revocable or irrevocable	
Powers granted to trustee	Scope of trustee's discretion; trustee's power to distribute principal and income
Manner and timetable of income and principal distribution to beneficiaries	Conditions and limitations on the distribution of assets; spendthrift provisions; sprinkling provisions
Description of assets transferred to trustee (unless trust is unfunded)	

belongs instead to the borrower. Hence, income tax on its yield will be payable by the borrower, whom you have chosen specifically because he or she is in a substantially lower tax bracket.

At one time, interest-free loans could be used as a means of income-shifting between family members. For example, a child could have received an interest-free loan from a parent and then earned interest on the money—interest would have been taxed at the child's lower tax bracket rather than at the parent's higher bracket.

But Congress eliminated this tactic. Now, if an individual makes an interest-free loan to another person who invests it at a lower tax bracket, the IRS will "impute" interest to the lender at the going interest rate. For example, suppose a parent makes an interest-free loan of $5,000, payable on demand, to a child, who invests the money in his name in a certificate of deposit. If the short-term U.S. Treasury interest rate is 4%, then the IRS will impute interest to the parent of 4% × $5,000 = $200. This amount will have to be included in the taxable income of the parent and is deductible by the child. Effectively, this undoes the tax-shifting of the interest-free loan.

For loans made at a below-market interest rate, a similar provision applies. In this case, the difference between the going Treasury rate and the interest actually charged will be imputed to the lender.

These rules apply to interest-free loans made in order to shift income to a lower tax bracket. For other interest-free loans, where the avoidance of tax is not *"one of the principal purposes,"* the rules are different. In such a case, you can make up to $100,000 of loans to an individual without the imputed interest rules coming into play. (For example, parents could lend money interest-free to an adult child to buy a home, attend school, etc.) In this situation, if the borrower does earn some income on the money, interest can still be imputed to the lender. The amount imputed is either the going Treasury rate or the actual amount of income earned, whichever is lower. However, no interest is imputed if the borrower's net investment income (from all sources) for the year is less than $1,000. This $1,000 exemption as well as the use of actual income earned instead of the Treasury rate applies only if tax-avoidance is not one of the principal purposes of the loan.

Also, if the total balance of amounts you lend to an individual does not exceed $10,000 and the loans are *not directly attributable to the purchase or carrying of income-producing assets*, then no income is imputed to you. This $10,000 limit and the $1,000 limit in the preceding paragraph are the same for married couples as for individuals; they are not doubled.

The rules above apply to loans made after June 6, 1984. However, for demand loans (i.e., loans without a predetermined maturity date), these rules apply no matter when the loans were made.

All states impose a *statute of limitation* on such transactions, usually four to six years. This means that the loan must have at least one installment paid (or must be repaid or renegotiated) within the statutory period. This presents no great problem if you keep an eye on the calendar, but if the time limit elapses without such action, the loan is uncollectible and the lender is regarded as having made a gift of the full amount to the borrower.

If an attempt to collect an interest-free loan is unsuccessful, the lender may be able to claim an income tax deduction for an uncollectible debt, but in order to convince the IRS of the legitimacy of this deduction he is likely to have to make bona fide efforts to collect it — perhaps by filing a lawsuit against the borrower.

Although the interest-free loan can shift income tax liability from the lender to the borrower, it does little or nothing to reduce your exposure to federal estate tax because the money will eventually be returned to you. If you should die while a loan of $25,000 is outstanding, your estate has not been reduced by $25,000 because it includes the promissory note for $25,000, although your personal representative may be able to persuade the IRS that the market value of an interest-free note is perhaps only 60% or 70% of its face value. On the other hand, the personal representative is responsible for making every effort to collect the loan, since the loan is considered part of your estate's assets.

IRREVOCABLE TRUSTS

Revocable trusts, despite their many advantages, do not relieve the grantor of liability for income tax or his estate from liability for federal estate tax on trust assets. If you are concerned about reducing your tax burden, you may want to consider an irrevocable trust. An irrevocable trust can serve all the purposes of a revocable trust, but the trust itself—or its beneficiaries if trust funds are distributed—pays the taxes on its income, usually at a lower rate than you would. The trust also offers possible relief from federal estate tax.

This tax relief, however, has a number of rather stringent conditions attached to it. Once you have set up an irrevocable trust, you may never change it, and any assets you transfer into such a trust pass out of your ownership permanently. You may never use either the principal or the income of such a trust for your own benefit, or to pay your debts, or to support a dependent whom you are legally obligated to support. Although you may serve as a trustee, your powers are limited to management of the assets; you are not permitted to make any changes that might affect the interests of the beneficiaries. In short, far more assuredly than diamonds, an irrevocable trust is "forever."

Despite the attractiveness of income-tax relief, most people of moderate means cannot afford to part forever with a substantial part of their assets. Indeed, irrevocable trusts of any significant size are used almost exclusively by the very rich, who make up probably less than one percent of American families. There are, however, some "mini" forms of irrevocable trust—the custodial account for minors and the trust for minors—that are used commonly by middle- to upper-middle-income persons to avoid taxes and to provide for the future needs of their children or grandchildren.

Custodial Account for Minors

Authorized by the Uniform Gifts to Minors Act or the Uniform Transfer to Minors Act, one or the other of which has been adopted by all states, a custodial account for minors is a simple, informal, and cost-free device for making gifts to minors, usually one's children, grandchildren, or other relatives. These gifts can take the form of bank accounts, money market accounts, securities, mutual funds, and, in states that have adopted the Uniform Transfers to Minors Act, life insurance policies, other kinds of personal property, and real estate. The gifts may be of any value, and they may be made cumulatively. That is, the donor can open a custodial account for a child in a very modest amount and add to it in any amount as frequently as he or she chooses.

Funds in a custodial account can be shifted from one form of investment to another as long as they are not removed from the custodianship or used for the benefit of anyone except the minor. There is no limit, moreover, to the number of accounts that a donor can establish for one minor, to the number of minors for which one donor can open accounts, or to the number of donors who can open an account for the same minor.

Simple though it is, the custodial account has two of the characteristics of an irrevocable trust. First, the custodian, who functions much as does the trustee of a formal irrevocable trust, may not use the funds for his own benefit and is legally responsible for safeguarding them and investing them prudently for the exclusive benefit of the minor. Second, the gift or gifts made to the account are irrevocable; for this reason any income tax on its yield is payable by the minor, not the donor.

Establishing a custodial account involves nothing more than obtaining a Social Security number for the minor and filling out a signature card at a bank (see Figure 7) or opening an account with a mutual fund or a brokerage firm. Like many parents and grandparents, you may decide to use such an account to accumulate funds for the minor's college education or some similar long-term goal. This may be preferable to accumulating the money in your own account, because the minor pays the income tax on the yield and is likely, especially in the early years, to be in the zero tax bracket.

There are, however, some important differences between the custodial account for minors and a formal irrevocable trust. Whereas

Figure 7
BANK ACCOUNT CARD:
CUSTODIAL ACCOUNT FOR MINOR

GIFT TRANSFER

I hereby deliver $_____ to Capitol Savings and Loan Association, a Michigan corporation for credit to an Optional Savings Account in the said institution in the

name of_____
                                    Name of Custodian

as Custodian for_____
                                    Name of Minor

under the Michigan Uniform Gifts to Minors Act.

This gift of money to the minor named, which gift shall be deemed to include all earnings thereon and any future additions thereto, is irrevocable and is made in accordance with and to include all the provisions of the said Statute of this State as it is now or hereafter may be amended.

_____   _____
            Date   Signature of Donor

NOTE: The use of this Gift Transfer Form is optional; however, it is recommended that it be used. The Donor and the Custodian may be the same person.

(front side)

Date_____   Account No._____

_____
    Last Name of Custodian   First Name   Middlle Name

as Custodian for_____
              Last Name of Minor   First Name   Middle Name

under the Michigan Uniform Gifts to Minors Act, hereby makes application for membership in the

CAPITOL SAVINGS AND LOAN ASSOCIATION

and for the issuance of an Optional Savings Account subject to the Laws of the State of Michigan, the rules and regulations of the Savings and Loan supervisory authority of the State of Michigan and the Articles of Incorporation and By-Laws of the Association, as they now are or as they may hereafter be amended.

_____as Custodian for
                            Signature

_____ under the
                      Name of Minor

Michigan Uniform Gifts to Minors Act.
Custodian Savings Account for Minor under "Michigan Uniform Gifts to Minors Act".
There can only be 1 custodian and 1 minor.

Form 149 2M 10-67

(back side)

a formal irrevocable trust can specify the age at which a beneficiary may get control of the funds and the conditions he must meet in order to get them, a custodial account permits no such restrictions; the minor automatically gains control of the account when he or she reaches majority—in most states, at the age of eighteen. Thus, on his eighteenth birthday, your child may, if he chooses, use the money to buy a $25,000 sports car rather than a freshman year at an Ivy League college and there is no way in which you can prevent his using the money in this way.

Moreover, neither the principal nor the income from a custodial account may be used for goods and services that the child's parents are obligated to provide. Money in a custodial account may, for example, be used for music lessons, summer camp, a new bicycle, or other "special" items but not for the child's food, clothing, medical care, or similar day-to-day expenses typically viewed as parental obligations.

Although the custodial account relieves the donor of income taxes on income generated by the gifted money, the deposits into the account may be subject to federal gift tax, since each deposit constitutes a gift. Normally, this is not a problem because annual gifts of $10,000 (or $20,000 with the consent of the donor's spouse) are not subject to this tax. But if the donor is also the custodian, the account balance as of the donor's death will be included in his estate for estate tax purposes should he die before the minor reaches the age of majority. For this reason, it may be advisable for the donor not to serve as the custodian. The donor might, for example, name his wife as custodian; a donor grandparent might name either the child's father or mother.

The simplest form of custodial account is a bank account opened in the name of "Mary Smith, Custodian for William Smith, Jr., under the Uniform Gifts to Minors Act (or Uniform Transfers to Minors Act) [your state]." An initial deposit of $10 to $25 will open a passbook account to which you can add at any time, or a larger amount can be used to buy a certificate of deposit. As the account increases in value through additional deposits or earned interest, you may decide to transfer the money into a brokerage or mutual fund account bearing the same title as the bank account. Either of these accounts carries the minor's Social Security number, and the minor is responsible for all taxes on its yield. Bear in mind, however, that once you deposit money into such an account it is an irrevocable gift and you can never again use it for your own purposes.

Tax on Children's Income

Special rules now apply to children under the age of 14. Under these rules, unearned income in excess of $1,200 is taxed at the parent's rate rather than at the child's rate. These rules were designed by Congress to prevent large-scale income-shifting to young children. As a result, current taxes are no longer saved when property producing income in excess of $1,200 is transferred to a child under age 14.

Moreover, a child cannot claim a personal exemption if he is eligible to be claimed as a dependent on a parent's tax return. This means that lower levels of income will be subject to income tax than before. In particular, only the first $600 of unearned income is now exempt from tax. Amounts between $600 and $1,200 are taxed at the child's rate (15% for 1993). The remainder of unearned income may be subject to tax at the parent's rate, depending upon whether or not the child is under age 14.

Although large-scale income-shifting to young children has been eliminated, this does not mean that income-shifting is totally ineffective. Under the 1993 tax tables, the tax on unearned income of $1,200 would be only $90, no doubt less than if taxed at the parent's higher tax bracket.

The income of a child age 14 or older is still taxed at the child's rate. Only children under age 14 are affected by the rule taxing unearned income at the parent's rate. Thus, income-shifting to an older child or other relative remains intact. Further, by choosing appropriate investments, advantage can be taken of the potential for income-shifting to an older child, even if the child is currently under age 14. This is done by choosing investments that pay off in future years in which the child will be at least age 14. One example of such an investment would be U.S. Series EE savings bonds. The interest on these bonds need not be reported until the year in which the bonds are redeemed, which can be arranged to occur after the child has reached age 14.

The Trust for Minors

If you like the concept of a custodial account but feel uncomfortable about the prospect of the minor's getting control of the assets at age 18 or 21, you may want to consider a formal trust for minors, known also as a Section 2503(c) trust (a reference to the section of the Internal Revenue Code that authorizes it). There are four differences between a custodial account and a trust for minors. First, under a trust for minors, the minor does not get control of the trust assets until at least age 21. Second, at age 21 the beneficiary may, if he chooses, extend the life of the trust indefinitely in order to take advantage of the trustee's responsible (and perhaps highly productive) management. Third, a trust for minors can be drafted to include several minors instead of only one. And, lastly, trust assets may include real estate as well as any type of personal property.

As in the case of a custodial account, any tax on income generated by the assets in a trust for minors, if distributed to the minor, is payable at the minor's rate as long as the child is at least age 14 and the distributions are not used to discharge your legal obligations (as a parent) to support the child. However, your contributions, if they exceed the annual, $10,000/$20,000 annual gift tax exclusion, may be subject to federal gift tax.

Your choice of trustee for a trust for minors should be based on the nature and the value of the trust assets. There is nothing to prevent you from serving as trustee (perhaps with your spouse as co-trustee), but if the trust assets are complex or of substantial value, you may decide that a professional trustee is a better choice.

The Full-fledged Irrevocable Trust

An irrevocable trust can be just as versatile as the revocable trust and can be established to serve the same purposes. The most important difference, aside from irrevocability, is that income tax on the yield from trust assets is payable not by the grantor but by the trust itself or by the beneficiaries if they receive periodic distributions, in either case presumably at a lower rate than what the grantor would pay. In addition, funds transferred to an irrevocable trust are completely unreachable by the grantor's creditors because they in fact no longer belong to the grantor. However, because the grantor can make no changes once the trust has been established, the trust document must be drafted with the greatest care and the choice of trustees must be made as judiciously as possible.

TRUSTS AND THE PROTECTION OF BENEFICIARIES

We have emphasized the use of trusts to avoid probate and to reduce income taxes and, in some circumstances, to reduce federal estate tax. These advantages, however, are incidental to the fundamental purpose of a trust: to carry on, after the grantor's death, his efforts to ensure the welfare of his designated beneficiaries.

As we have noted, transferring assets through a will or through joint ownership gives immediate and unconditional control of them to a surviving beneficiary who, for one reason or another, may not be able to conserve them, increase them, or use them wisely. Transferring them by means of a trust, on the other hand, can do much to protect the assets against loss or dissipation, to ensure that they are used in ways of which you would approve, and thus to promote your designated beneficiary's long-term welfare.

If, for example, your wife is inexperienced or simply uninterested in managing assets of substantial value or complex makeup, a professional trustee is more likely to protect or increase them than she is. But even if she is both capable and motivated, she may be unable to resist the importunate demands from relatives, friends, and suitors that many widows face when they inherit large sums of money. In such a situation, a professional trustee can serve as a buffer.

A trust can also protect the interests of your children, both minor and adult. Most parents ensure the welfare of minor children by designating in their wills a guardian or, if a substantial inheritance is involved, two guardians: a *guardian of the person* and a *guardian of the property*, the latter also sometimes known as a conservator. A serious limitation of this arrangement is that the guardian or the conservator must manage the child's inheritance under the strict supervision of the probate court, and courts are often both conservative and inflexible in their supervision. Moreover, these arrangements terminate automatically when the child reaches the age of majority, regardless of the child's ability or inclination to manage what he or she may consider a windfall. If, however, you establish a trust for the children, the trustee serves the function of the conservator, free from supervision by the probate court and able to exercise as much discretion as you provide in the trust document and for as long as you wish to postpone the ultimate distribution of your estate.

A conservatorship automatically terminates when the child reaches the age of majority (18 in most states), but even "adult" children may require protection against their own immaturity or irresponsibility, especially if large sums of money are involved. For example, if an adult child of yours seems to believe that money is something that should be spent immediately on whatever catches his eye, you might consider incorporating in your trust a *spendthrift* provision, which instructs the trustee to dole out the assets in limited amounts–for necessities only, perhaps—and which prohibits the beneficiary from selling his future income from the trust (usually at a deep discount) to various financial institutions that buy such interests. Alternatively, you might incorporate an *incentive* provision, under which the amount of each payment to the beneficiary is linked to income that the beneficiary earns through his own efforts.

Often, money left to adult children may be dissipated not by the children themselves but by their spouses, especially if a divorce occurs shortly after receipt of the inheritance. This can be averted and the money kept in the family by drafting the trust document so that the inheritance, or a part of it, goes directly to the children of the marriage. If an adult child's marriage seems currently unstable, the trust can be drafted so that no payments are made until the instability has been resolved.

Given sufficient discretion, a trustee can cope with problems that you cannot foresee at the time you set up the trust, such as sharp differences in the affluence of your children, or severe financial stress suffered by one of them years after your death. If you establish a *sprinkling* trust, the trustee, instead of distributing predetermined shares of assets or income to each child, can alter the shares to meet each child's current needs and can shift distribution from one beneficiary to another as these needs change.

A sprinkling trust provision can be useful even when no financial crisis is involved. Suppose, for example, that a grandchild needs $20,000 for a year of college tuition. If the trust were to pay the trust income of $20,000 to the child's father, who is in the 31% tax bracket, the child would receive only $13,800 after the father had paid income tax on this amount. If, instead, the trustee had the discretion to pay the $20,000 of trust income directly to the child, the loss through taxation would be significantly less.

Each of the strategies we have discussed enables you to have your wishes carried out years and possibly decades after your death. All of them, however, embody an obvious risk: that "the dead hand of the past"—your own—will constrict or even damage the lives of your surviving beneficiaries. It is therefore important to recognize that some of your beneficiaries, because they are more than a quarter of a century younger than you, live in a different world from yours, face different problems, and have different standards and aspirations. Too rigid a trust document may protect your assets but may cripple the very people whom the assets are intended to benefit.

C H A P T E R 5

OWNERSHIP BY THE CLOSELY HELD CORPORATION

The forms of ownership described in the preceding chapters are available to almost anyone who finds them advantageous. Another form of ownership—the closely held corporation—cannot be used by everybody. But if you meet the qualifications for incorporating, which are not unreasonably stringent, you may find the closely held corporation by far the most effective form of ownership for at least some of your assets as well as for part or all of your current earnings.

Briefly, here are some of the advantages you may gain by incorporating:

Income earned by a corporation is taxed by the IRS at a rate of only 15% on the first $25,000 and 18% on the next $25,000, a far lower rate than you would be taxed if you were to earn the same amount as an individual.

If you capitalize your corporation with common stock that you own in another domestic corporation—e.g., your 100 shares of IBM—you may exclude 70% of the IBM dividends from federal income tax and pay a sharply reduced rate on the remaining 30%.

Your corporation can provide you with liberal health-care coverage, disability insurance, and other fringe benefits, the costs of which are tax-deductible by the corporation as a legitimate expense and tax-free to you.

Your corporation can pay (and tax-deduct) the premiums on a term life insurance policy for you with a face value of up to $50,000 payable to a beneficiary designated by you. A $5,000 death benefit can be paid tax-free to an employee's beneficiary and deducted by the corporation.

Incorporation may permit you to control your income so as to reduce your current income taxes or, once you retire, to avoid exceeding the earnings limitations imposed by the Social Security Administration.

By giving shares of your corporation to your spouse, your children, or other intended beneficiaries, you may be able to avoid probate and to avoid or reduce federal estate tax.

Your corporation may reduce your housing costs by paying you for the space it occupies in your home. Or, conversely, the corporation may own your home, charge you rent for the space you occupy, and gain a tax advantage by doing so.

If you sell your home, your corporation can offer your buyer either a land contract or a mortgage and will pay income tax on the resulting interest at a lower tax rate than you.

If you use an automobile for corporation business, the corporation can buy and maintain one for you, deducting all costs and depreciation as a corporate expense.

Like some types of trust, a corporation is legally immortal. It can survive your death and continue to function, uninterrupted by the probate process or by a change in the identity of its shareholders.

Because a corporation is a separate entity, you cannot be held personally responsible for its debts and other liabilities beyond your initial investment. Similarly, the corporation's assets are not vulnerable to the claims of your personal creditors.

Just as not everyone can qualify to establish a corporation, so not all these advantages are available or even relevant to everyone who incorporates. But if you find even a few of them attractive, you may conclude that they are well worth the effort of establishing and operating a corporation of your own.

CORPORATIONS, LARGE VS. SMALL

As you may recall from your economics course, a corporation is a legal entity that is entitled to conduct business as though it were a person. Unlike a person, however, it is immortal and it is owned and controlled by a group of human shareholders, who are entitled to a share of its profits, although they cannot be held personally liable for its losses beyond their investment in the corporation's stock. A public corporation's shares are traded daily on one or more stock exchanges, and virtually anyone can buy these shares in whatever number he can afford.

This textbook definition usually brings to mind General Motors or IBM or any other of the huge Fortune 500 corporations. But the fact is that the special advantages enjoyed by corporations are available not only to huge enterprises operating with vast amounts of capital but also to individuals who incorporate primarily for the sake of tax relief, estate-planning advantages, and flexibility in managing both the income they earn and the assets they already own.

Twenty years ago, these advantages were recognized mainly by superstar athletes and other millionaire celebrities—or, rather, by their tax accountants. Then doctors, dentists, lawyers, and other high-income professionals began to form "professional corporations" (see p. 93). Today, however, many people with more moderate net worth and earnings are coming to recognize the same advantages and are discovering that setting up a small corporation is well worth the effort and expense.

The rest of this chapter is not intended as a guide for those planning to raise capital for an ambitious business enterprise. Instead, it will describe a special type of corporation, the *closely held* corporation, which is suitable for people interested mainly in gaining corporate advantages with respect to money they now earn or intend to earn largely through their own business efforts.

Although the closely held corporation enjoys all the advantages of the large, public corporation—and some others in addition—it differs from General Electric or Exxon in a number of important ways:

Shares of the closely held corporation are not offered to the general public or traded on any stock exchange. Instead, its shareholders tend to be a few people, usually members of the same family or close friends. In many such corporations, all shares are held by husband and wife, although a small number may be held by children and other relatives.

Most, if not all, of the shareholders are also directors or officers of the corporation and are usually its sole, or at least its most important, employees. In most such corporations a controlling interest (51% of all outstanding stock) is owned by one person or by a married couple. In fact, in some closely held corporations, one person owns all the stock and functions as the corporation's sole director, officer, and employee.

Although shareholders' meetings must be held at least annually, these can be very informal affairs, held over the dinner table or on the patio. At such meetings, decisions regarding dividend payments, salary adjustments, fringe benefits, and other policy matters can usually be made swiftly and easily, because the shareholders are few in number and are less likely to have conflicting interests.

Although the closely held corporation may at any one time derive its earnings from one particular kind of service or product, its corporate charter can specify that it is entitled to engage in virtually any kind of business activity. In short, it can be every bit as flexible as its huge conglomerate counterparts.

The closely held corporation can be capitalized for relatively little money; in fact, some states require no minimum paid-in capital at the outset.

As you can see, then, not only in size but also in structure, capitalization, and formality of operation, the closely held corporation is more like a cottage industry than the mammoth organization we usually think of as "the American corporation." And its corporate headquarters may fit comfortably in your own cottage.

WHO MAY INCORPORATE?

In the United States, any adult can go into business for himself or set up a partnership without much concern about rules and regulations. Corporations, however, because they enjoy special privileges, are closely regulated by the states and scrutinized rather carefully by the IRS. Hence, before you succumb to the attractions of incorporating, you ought first to review the following eligibility requirements.

Source of Corporate Income

Because a corporation is a business enterprise, the law requires it to earn a substantial part of its income from the direct efforts of its employees. This may seem too obvious to deserve mention but some people, eager to gain the tax advantages stemming from incorporation, assume that they can capitalize a corporation with securities for the sole purpose of enjoying the tax advantage on their yield. Such a corporation, which has no intention of operating as a business, is known as a "personal holding company" and its "passive" income from investments and similar sources is taxed by the IRS at the punitive rate of 50%.

This does not mean that you may not capitalize your corporation with securities you own, or that your corporation may not use its cash reserves to buy and sell securities in its own name. Indeed, as we shall see shortly, the tax exemption enjoyed by corporations on income they receive from the stock they own in other corporations is one of the reasons why the closely held corporation is attractive to people of moderate means. But if the "personal holding company" tax penalty is to be avoided, a corporation's income from investments may not exceed 59% of its total income. The rest must be earned from the actual operation of the corporation business — presumably by the efforts of you and/or your fellow shareholders. These corporate earnings may consist of money you now earn as an unincorporated individual from any of a variety of full-time or part-time activities — from consulting, from patents or royalties, from work as an unsalaried real estate salesperson, or even from dealing in stamps as a philatelist.

Once you incorporate, all you need do is ask your customers or clients to make their payments to your corporation instead of you — to John Smith, Inc., instead of to plain John Smith. People to whom you render service as an "independent contractor" rather than as a regular employee are likely to be perfectly willing to pay your corporation for your services and to regard you as one of the corporation's employees.

This arrangement is feasible even when only one employee of the corporation is capable of providing a service or a product. A writer or a commercial artist, for example, can have her royalties or fees made payable to her corporation simply by signing an agreement with her publisher or client stipulating that the work will be done entirely by her. This general rule does not hold, however, for physicians, lawyers, and certain other professionals who are licensed or regulated by the state; these individuals are limited to a special form of corporation, the professional corporation, discussed in the next section.

If, however, your sole source of income is a regular salary, it is doubtful that your employer would agree to change your status from employee to independent contractor. In fact, such a change might work to your personal disadvantage, since an independent contractor, unlike an employee, receives no fringe benefits and no employer contributions to Social Security, unemployment insurance, workers' compensation insurance, or pension plans. If, then, you are on an employer's payroll, you can form a corporation only if other employees of your corporation (your spouse, for example, or your children) can generate income for the corporation.

Scope of Corporate Activities

Although you may have clearly in mind a source of current or future corporate income, there is no need for your corporate charter to specify it. That is, if you intend to earn money from financial consulting, the charter need not describe the purpose of the corporation as "financial consultation." Instead, the charter should be as broad as possible, permitting the corporation in the future to engage in any activity except one that requires licensing—optometry, for example—or a state charter or franchise, such as banking.

Number of Directors

All but two states and the District of Columbia permit one individual to establish a corporation and to serve simultaneously as all of its shareholders, directors, officers, and employees (see Table 6). But if more than one incorporator or director is required, you can name as the others your spouse, other family members, or close friends. You may also designate yourself as the registered agent and list your home address as the registered office.

Furthermore, you are free to apply for your corporate charter in any state, no matter where your corporation is actually located or where it carries on its principal business. There are, however, additional costs involved in forming a "foreign" corporation, as well as the requirement of registering it to do business in your home state.

Minimum Capitalization

Some states require that a corporation be capitalized initially, but this capitalization need not be in the form of cash. Securities, real estate, mortgages, furniture, office equipment, and even the past labor of its incorporators can constitute all or part of the capitalization.

TWO SPECIAL TYPES OF CORPORATION

The requirements outlined above apply generally to all closely held corporations. Two special types of corporation, however—the professinal corporation and the "S corporation"—have distinctive features that warrant further discussion.

The Professional Corporation

Until recently, licensed professionals such as physicians, lawyers, accountants, and engineers were not allowed to incorporate their practices. Today, however, all states permit them to form a *professional corporation* (in some states called a professional association or professional service corporation), and today large numbers of professionals enjoy the usual advantages available to corporations: tax-free health insurance, tax-sheltered pension plans, profit-sharing arrangements, and other tax-free fringe benefits.

But although the professional corporation resembles other closely held corporations in many ways, state and federal laws impose on it a number of special restrictions that do not apply to closely held corporations not involved in professional practice.

Unlike the conventional business corporation, the professional corporation may be formed only by licensed individuals practicing the same profession, and no unlicensed individuals may buy, hold, or inherit its shares. Moreover, in some states the corporate name may not be fictitious or fabricated but usually must include the name of at least one of the licensed practitioners. "John Smith, M.D., P.C.," for example, is acceptable but "Quikcure, Inc." is not.

More important, the principle of limited personal liability does not apply fully to the professional corporation. Patients or clients retain the right to file malpractice suits against any individual member of the corporation, not merely against the corporation itself. However, one shareholder cannot be held responsible for judgments rendered against a fellow shareholder, as he can in a professional partnership.

Furthermore, by incorporating, the shareholders in a professional corporation lose their Fifth Amendment rights with respect to corporate activities. That is, in the course of an IRS audit they may not refuse to supply information on grounds of self-incrimination. The principle of confidentiality with respect to patients or clients, however, remains intact.

Unlike the conventional corporation, which may be formed to engage in a number of enterprises, the professional corporation is limited to practice of the specified profession. Although it may own the building it occupies and any vehicles and other equipment essential to the practice, it may not own other investments with a view to tax-sheltering their income. In addition, the salaries that shareholders may draw must be "reasonable" in the eyes of the IRS, on the grounds that salaries are tax-deductible by the corporation. There is no limit on dividends, however, because the corporation pays taxes on its income before the dividends are paid and the recipient is taxed on them as well.

The requirement that every shareholder must be a licensed professional can seriously limit the usefulness of the professional corporation with respect to estate planning. Because shares may not be held by family members or bequeathed to beneficiaries through a will or trust unless they are licensed professionals, the shares of a stockholder who dies must be purchased by the corporation or by one of its surviving shareholders. In such circumstances the value of the shares may be difficult to determine, because book value—that is, the value of the corporation's assets—rarely reflects the actual value of shares. These difficulties are usually overcome by means of a shareholders' agreement that specifies how share value is to be determined as well as how, when, and by whom the stock is to be purchased upon the retirement or death of a shareholder.

The fact that large numbers of professionals have incorporated would indicate that the advantages of a professional corporation apparently outweigh its limitations. But in one survey, professionals who chose not to incorporate responded that their income did not justify the time, trouble, and expense involved. Because the professional corporation, like any other closely held corporation, involves accounting, legal, and other expenses, the decision to incorporate requires careful thought—preferably in consultation with a tax accountant and a lawyer skilled in business law.

The "S Corporation"

Another special type of closely held corporation, named the "S corporation" after the section of the Internal Revenue Code that authorizes it, differs in one important respect from the conventional corporation. This difference makes it attractive for a small number of people in special circumstances but of little or no interest to the vast majority.

The distinguishing feature is that the S corporation pays no corporate income tax. Instead, each shareholder reports his share of corporate profits or losses on his individual income tax return, as in the tax treatment of a partnership. The shareholders need not actually receive their share of the profits in cash, but instead may leave the money in the corporation as cash reserve or working capital. But whether or not they actually receive the income, the shareholders must pay income tax on it for the year in which the corporation received it.

Although the corporate income tax rate is generally lower than the individual tax rate, there are several reasons why some people prefer to have all corporate profits taxed as individual income. First, their individual income tax bracket may, in fact, be even lower than the corporate tax rate, or they may be able to reduce their individual income tax by deducting losses sustained by the corporation. Second, they avoid double taxation on dividends, which normally are taxable both as corporate profits when earned and as income when received by the shareholder. Third, investment tax credits on corporate purchases of certain property can be "passed through" to the stockholders and claimed on their individual tax returns. Lastly, they can enjoy the income-tax-free fringe benefits that only a corporation can provide on a tax-deductible basis.

Because individual income tax is payable by the recipient of all salaries and dividends, the IRS is not concerned that the level of salaries paid be reasonably equivalent to salaries prevailing in the industry, not will it penalize the corporation for accumulating an excessive level of cash reserves, as it may penalize conventional corporations. This makes it possible for the officers of an S corporation to manipulate salaries, dividends, and cash reserves with considerable freedom and flexibility.

This type of corporation may be especially useful if you would like to distribute corporate income to your children. If you give them stock and have the corporation pay dividends, their dividend income remains in the family but is taxable to the children, who presumably are in a much lower tax bracket than you. As to unearned income received by children under age 14, see p. 83.

Although the S corporation may engage in any type of business, all of its dividend income is fully taxable. This makes it less effective as a dividend sheltering device than the conventional corporation, which is permitted to exclude from taxes 70% of its dividend income from other domestic corporations. Moreover, many fringe benefits that can be provided by a conventional corporation are not available to an S corporation. In addition, the IRS imposes the following restrictions on the S corporation.

It may be formed only in those states that recognize it, and it must be an American company.

It is limited to 35 shareholders, all of whom generally must be individuals (rather than corporations or trusts). Hence, if any shareholder transfers his shares into a trust, the corporation will lose its "S" status and may be heavily penalized by the IRS.

None of its shareholders may be a nonresident alien.

It must not belong to an affiliated group of corporations.

It may have only one class of stock outstanding.

Because the advantages of an S corporation depend very heavily on your personal financial situation and your future plans, it should not be chosen without thorough consultation with a competent tax advisor. Whatever decision you make, however, is not irrevocable. With the consent of all stockholders, it is possible for a conventional corporation to change to "S" form and vice versa.

If your reading of the foregoing pages leads you to conclude that your own situation qualifies you for incorporation, your decision to do so will depend on your assessment of the benefits it offers you.

Before describing the procedure for establishing the corporation, therefore, we shall examine both the advantages and the costs in some detail.

TAX ADVANTAGES OF INCORPORATION

The income tax advantages of incorporation stem not from any intricate tax sheltering maneuvers that the corporate structure permits but from the simple fact that the IRS has traditionally treated corporate income much more liberally than income earned by individuals. A corporation earning $50,000 in net profits, for example, pays federal income tax at the rate of only 15%, and on the next $25,000 at only 25%. Hence, your corporation will retain more after-tax earnings than you would as an individual because your personal tax bracket on $50,000 of income would be substantially higher.

Of course, transferring corporate earnings from the corporation to your pocket can be done only if the corporation pays you a salary (on which you will be taxed but which the corporation deducts as an expense) or if it pays you a dividend (on which both you and the corporation will be taxed at your respective rates). But a great advantage of the corporate structure is that earnings can be retained by the corporation as a reserve, be reinvested, and be paid out to you at rates and at times that are most advantageous to your personal tax situation.

At the time of this writing, for example, a corporation is entitled to accumulate a reserve of $250,000—or $150,000 if it is engaged solely in personal service—without attracting the attention of the IRS. After you retire, at which time your tax bracket is likely to be lower than it is today, this reserve can be paid to you as salary or as dividends. Or you may decide to dissolve the corporation and distribute its assets, in which case your proceeds are taxable as long-term capital gains.

But the low tax rate on corporate earnings is not the whole story. One little-known tax advantage enjoyed by corporations is that they are permitted to own stock in other domestic corporations and that 70% of the dividends earned from this stock is not subject to income tax. If, then, you set up a corporation and capitalize it with common stock (or use the cash with which you capitalize it to buy stock for the corporation) your tax savings could be substantial.

Suppose, for example, that you personally own 100 shares of AT&T and that your annual dividend income is $540. If you are in the 31% tax bracket and if you have already used up the exclusion on the first $200 of dividends, you will pay a federal income tax of $167.40 on this dividend. If, however, the stock is owned by your corporation, 70% of the $540 is excluded from taxation and your corporation, depending on its other income, may be taxed at the rate of only 15% on the remaining $162—that is, the corporate income tax would be only $24.30. Provided that dividend or other "passive" income does not exceed 59% of the corporation's earnings, holding stock in the corporate name is a legitimate and highly effective way of reducing income tax. Bear in mind, however, that you cannot use this corporate income personally until the corporation pays it to you in the form of either salary or dividends, both of which will increase your personal tax liability.

Corporations are not eligible for the tax deferment currently available to individuals who reinvest their dividends in certain public utility stocks. In general, financial advisors suggest that corporations invest in high-yield common stocks of domestic corporations whose dividends are fully taxable.

Fringe benefits provided by the corporation to its employees are tax-deductible by the corporation as a business expense but are not usually taxable to the recipient. Medical, dental, and optical benefits provide a convenient example. Currently, if your family's health insurance premiums and medical bills run to $5,000 a year, you may deduct only that portion of them that exceeds 7.5% of your adjusted gross income. If, however, the directors of your corporation decide to pay 100 percent of their employees' medical costs, your entire medical bill would be tax-deductible by the corporation and tax-free to you.

Your corporation's medical fringe benefits may be as liberal as the directors choose. In addition to the usual benefits, they may provide unlimited coverage for prescription drugs and for dental, optometric, and psychiatric services for employees and their dependents—coverages that are often not provided at all by the benefit programs of large corporations. Bear in mind, however, that such a program generally must cover *all* employees and not merely the corporate officers. That can become rather expensive if your corporation eventually hires a large staff.

Other fringe benefits that a corporation may provide for its employees include a pension plan, death benefits, disability income insurance, life insurance, loans with attractive interest rates, payment of employees' legal fees, membership in a health club or country club, travel expenses to explore new business possibilities or to attend business-related seminars, and purchase of a vacation retreat for the use of its key employees.

OTHER ADVANTAGES

Limited Liability

One widely known advantage of the corporate form is the protection it provides against personal liability. This means that individual stockholders cannot be held personally liable (beyond their original investment) for any debts or liabilities incurred by the corporation or for claims resulting from successful lawsuits against the corporation or other shareholders. In this respect a corporation is quite different from a partnership, in which each partner is personally liable to the full extent of his net worth for business debts incurred by his partner(s) and for damage claims against his partner(s) stemming from partnership business.

For the closely held corporation, however, this advantage is probably more theoretical than real. Although it may offer some protection if the corporation is vulnerable to product-liability or negligence claims, and although it safeguards the shareholders' personal assets in case the corporation goes bankrupt through bad luck or poor management, it is not likely to offer effective protection against creditors, simply because no sensible lender or vendor will offer credit to a closely held corporation until it has established a satisfactory credit rating. When a closely held corporation without a credit rating applies for credit, its officers are likely to be asked to guarantee or cosign the debt—in which case the corporate limitation on liability is of no consequence.

Estate Planning

Of far greater advantage to shareholders are the possibilities for estate planning provided by their ownership of shares. As a shareholder, you may transfer any number of shares you own to anyone else during your lifetime or through your will or trust, although shares you give away during your lifetime may be subject to federal gift tax, shares you bequeath by will or trust may be subject to federal and state death taxes, and shares bequeathed by will must be probated.

Despite these considerations, transferring assets in the form of corporate stock offers you a number of options. As the controlling shareholder, you have the right to decide whether and when dividends are to be paid. Thus, if you like you can transfer to your children or other beneficiaries shares that, if the corporation declares no dividends, will have value only after your death. Or you can transfer shares and have your corporation declare periodic dividends on them so that your children can enjoy the income while you are still alive.

SOME COSTS AND DISADVANTAGES

The advantages of incorporating carry a price in terms of money, time, and attention. Although this price is difficult to quantify, and although you can to some extent reduce your money costs by do-it-yourself labor, you need to be aware that establishing and operating a corporation, even one that is closely held, entails at least some professional assistance as well as effort and attention on your part.

Start-up Costs

Starting a corporation involves, at the outset, making application for a charter from the state in which you incorporate. Although several books suggest that this is a do-it-yourself project and provide preprinted forms, the quality of these books is variable, to say the least. A far safer approach is to consult a lawyer with business law and tax experience, who can help you decide whether incorporation is advisable and who can tailor the corporate framework to your specific situation before filing an application for a certificate of incorporation.

Legal fees for this kind of service vary, but in most situations a fee of $500 to $1,500 should cover the services described in the following section on establishing your corporation. This fee also should cover the one-time state fee for processing the application, a set of printed stock certificates, a corporate seal, and a book for minutes and other records.

Continuing Costs

Because it is a separate entity, your corporation will be required to file its own federal and state income tax returns (including quarterly estimates) and a half-dozen or more periodic reports to various state agencies. In addition, it must periodically pay its share of Social Security contributions, unemployment insurance premiums and, in some cases, state workers' compensation insurance premiums for each of its employees. Hiring an accountant to take care of this paperwork will cost money, although the fees will be tax-deductible. Doing it yourself will take time and a certain amount of expertise.

Aside from filing additional tax returns and meeting increased operating costs, you will need to do an increased amount of book-keeping—perhaps much more meticulously than you do for your personal finances. Because the corporation is a separate entity, you are not permitted to co-mingle its funds with your own, and every penny of its income and expenditures must be reflected in written records.

In addition, formal minutes must be kept to record the decisions made at each directors' and shareholders' meeting, no matter how informal the meeting itself may have been. Sample minutes are shown in Figure 9, later in this chapter.

Whether or not you find these tasks and responsibilities onerous will depend on your personal interests and skills, and whether you find the inevitable out-of-pocket costs justifiable will depend on the advantages you anticipate. But both are unavoidable realities. We stress them here not to discourage you from incorporating but because many people, seduced by the apparent (and sometimes exaggerated) advantages of incorporation but unaware of the costs and effort it entails, plunge ahead, only to abandon the project after investing considerable time and money.

Determining Current Share Value

The fact that its shares are not traded publicly gives the closely held corporation a good deal of freedom. But because there is no daily market for its shares, the value of a share at any given time is difficult to assess.

This difficulty can to some extent be alleviated by specifying in a stockholders' agreement that the value of a share is to be based on "book" value—that is, the current value of all capital equipment, cash, accounts receivable, and inventory at the time the share value is to be determined. But for certain kinds of business—especially a personal-service business—book value may not provide a fair basis. In such situations the stockholders' agreement may specify that a share should be valued at five times the annual per share average earnings over the past three years or at an amount agreed to annually by the stockholders, or at an amount determined by a professional appraisal.

Buying and Selling Shares

Calculating the value of a share becomes important only when shares are to be bought or sold, but even when share value can be determined fairly the trading of closely held shares may involve further difficulties.

On the one hand, a shareholder—say, a child who has inherited some shares—may find them extremely difficult to dispose of because there is no daily market for them (as there is for publicly traded shares like AT&T, for example) and a potential buyer may have no reliable way of determining their value. On the other hand, if a shareholder does manage to sell shares to an outsider, the close-knit relationship among the original stockholders will be diluted, if not destroyed, and in some circumstances control of the corporation may pass out of their hands.

One way to avoid this difficulty is to specify a repurchase plan in a stockholders' agreement, which specifies that shares offered for sale must be offered first to the corporation, then to the remaining stockholders, and lastly to the general public. The problem of loss of control will be avoided, of course, if one person, or a stable marital couple, always retains at least 51 percent of the outstanding shares of stock.

Excessive Profits, Salaries, and Dividends

Although we have pointed out that you may be able to use a closely held corporation to manipulate both your assets and your income in ways that give you tax advantages, such manipulations can be done only within limits. The IRS is clearly aware of the various tax-reducing tactics available to incorporators, and hence it scrutinizes corporate returns rather carefully and provides penalties for certain excesses.

You may, for example, see a significant advantage in accumulating corporate profits, investing them on behalf of the corporation, and having the corporation pay income tax on their yield at a lower rate than you would if you were to invest them after receiving them as salary. But if you accumulate earnings of more than $250,000 (or $150,000 if yours is a personal-service corporation), the IRS may tax them at the rate of 27.5% on the first $100,000 of excess and 38.5% on the balance. This penalty is an additional tax on top of the normal corporate income tax. Hence, if your corporation's retained earnings approach the $150,000/$250,000 limit, it can avoid the tax by paying a dividend to its shareholders.

You may be able to convince the IRS that you have legitimate reasons for this accumulation: that you need funds for expansion or diversification, for increasing inventory or replacing obsolescing equipment, for buying or improving buildings, or for some other valid business purpose. But unless you actually have such a plausible reason, you risk a penalty if you allow profits to accumulate excessively instead of paying them out in salaries, fringe benefits, and dividends.

Similarly, although you can adjust your salary scale within certain broad limits, the IRS requires that it bear a reasonable resemblance to salaries paid for similar services in other companies. If your salary is too high, the IRS may interpret the excess as a disguised dividend, which you are paying yourself in the form of salary because salaries are tax-deductible by the corporation, whereas dividends are not.

You may, on the other hand, be tempted to pay yourself too low a salary in order to reduce your tax bracket or to avoid jeopardizing your Social Security retirement benefits. But here, too, you may have to convince the IRS that your salary is reasonable in terms of the services you provide. A salary that appears to be too low may be questioned not only by the IRS but also by the Social Security Administration. When you apply for retirement benefits, you will be asked whether you are, or are related to, a corporate officer. If so, you may be required to submit a financial statement so that your corporate salary can be compared to the overall earnings of the corporation.

As for dividends, the IRS takes the position that stockholders in a closely held corporation should be paid dividends on essentially the same basis as stockholders in large, public corporations—that is, that the amount and frequency of the dividends should bear a reasonable relationship to the current financial status and the future prospects of the corporation's business.

Dealing at Arm's Length

The fact that a corporation is a distinct entity—completely separate from you as an individual—means not only that you may not "borrow" money from it to tide you over an emergency but also that you may not use its funds to make personal loans or gifts to children or other relatives for any purpose. Similarly, although there is no objection to your hiring your children or other relatives, such employees must have bona fide jobs at reasonable rates of pay. Padding the payroll with dummy jobs is just as illegal in a corporation as in the U.S. Congress—and probably more likely to be detected and punished.

Occasions may arise when you might be tempted to involve the corporation in transactions that would benefit you personally. You may want the corporation to buy you a car for your personal use or to lend a relative money at a favorable rate of interest. But the IRS requires that all the business of a corporation be done "at arm's length"—that is, not with children or relatives or for the special personal advantage of its shareholders.

ESTABLISHING YOUR CORPORATION

There is no way in which a book can help you determine whether, given your particular financial situation, skills, and aspirations, incorporation would be advantageous to *you*. Our experience indicates that many people, tempted by the apparent advantages of incorporating, go ahead without a full understanding of the responsibilities involved, a clear perception of the state and federal regulations governing corporations, or a realistic view of their personal circumstances. Hence, even if the disadvantages described above have not discouraged you from incorporating, it is crucially important that you consult a tax accountant or a lawyer experienced in business and tax law before you proceed further. A frank and thorough consultation may change your mind in one direction or the other.

Although the procedures involved in establishing a corporation are essentially the same, regardless of the corporation's size or scope, in the case of the closely held corporation many of these procedures can be simplified, telescoped, or done very informally. For example, there may be no need for a shareholders' meeting to approve the directors' choice of officers, because usually the directors, the officers, and the shareholders are the same individuals. Similarly, corporate bylaws, which in a large corporation must be approved by a majority of the shareholders, can, in the case of the closely held corporation, be prepared by the lawyer handling the incorporation and quickly approved by the incorporators. For this reason, the discussion that follows is intended not as a detailed how-to-do-it guide but rather as a description of what-has-to-be-done.

This does not mean that you should simply ask your lawyer to establish a corporation for you and leave everything in his hands. Since a lawyer's fee for setting up a corporation is often based on the time he devotes to it, you can reduce your costs by thinking about the following issues before meeting with him. On a number of them, you will not be able to make firm decisions until conferring with him, but thinking about them ahead of time will reduce the time you both spend and increase the likelihood that he will address your particular needs.

State of Incorporation

The establishment of a corporation is regulated by state rather than federal law, and state requirements vary rather widely, from the severely restrictive to the highly permissive. These requirements specify, among other matters, the minimum initial capitalization, minimum number of directors, the number and kinds of stock that may be issued, the filing fees, and the number and kinds of periodic reports you must file.

If the regulations of your own state are too stringent, you can incorporate in a state more favorable to corporations—Nevada or Delaware, for example—since there is no requirement that you incorporate in the state in which you live or do business. Some of the more liberal states, however, require "foreign"—that is, out-of-state—corporations to maintain a resident agent there. Although many such agents offer their services to a large number of corporations for an annual fee, you may decide that this additional requirement makes out-of-state incorporation simply not worth the trouble. In general, unless you find your state's requirements too burdensome, or unless your corporation intends to expand significantly, your lawyer will probably advise incorporating in your own state. Regardless of the state of incorporation, your corporation will pay all state taxes to the state in which it does business.

Table 6
SELECTED STATE LAWS GOVERNING INCORPORATION

	Min. No. of Incorporators	Must Publish Articles	Min. Beginning Capital	Min. No. of Directors	Minimum Filing Fee	Name Reserv. Fee
Alabama	1	No	None	1	75	10
Alaska	1	No	None	1	150	No fee
Arizona	2	Yes	None	1	150	10
Arkansas	1	No	None	1	50	25
California	1	No	None	1	100	10
Colorado	1	No	None	1	50	10
Connecticut	1	No	$1,000	1	150	30
Delaware	1	No	None	1	25	10
D.C.	1	No	$1,000	3	100	25
Florida	1	No	None	1	35	35
Georgia	1	Yes	None	1	60	No fee
Hawaii	1	No	None	1	50	10
Idaho	1	No	None	1	100	20
Illinois	1	No	None	1	75	25
Indiana	1	No	None	1	90	20
Iowa	1	No	None	1	50	10
Kansas	1	No	None	1	75	No fee
Kentucky	1	No	None	1	40	15
Louisiana	1	No	None	1	50	20
Maine	1	No	None	1	75	20
Maryland	1	No	None	1	20	No fee
Massachusetts	1	No	None	1	200	15
Michigan	1	No	None	1	50	10
Minnesota	1	No	None	1	135	No fee
Mississippi	1	No	None	1	50	25

Missouri	1	No	None	1	50	20
Montana	1	No	None	1	50	No fee
Nebraska	1	Yes	None	1	40	15
Nevada	1	No	None	1	125	20
New Hampshire	1	No	None	1	35	15
New Jersey	1	No	None	1	100	50
New Mexico	1	No	$1,000	1	100	25
New York	1	No	None	1	135	20
North Carolina	1	No	None	1	100	10
North Dakota	1	No	None	1	80	10
Ohio	1	No	None	1	85	5
Oklahoma	1	No	None	1	50	5
Oregon	1	No	None	1	50	10
Pennsylvania	1	Yes	None	1	100	52
Rhode Island	1	No	None	1	150	50
South Carolina	1	No	None	1	10	10
South Dakota	1	No	$1,000	1	40	10
Tennessee	1	No	None	1	60	40
Texas	1	No	$1,000	1	300	40
Utah	3	No	$1,000	1	75	20
Vermont	1	No	None	1	25	10
Virginia	1	No	None	1	75	25
Washington	1	No	None	1	175	No fee
West Virginia	1	No	None	1	10	No fee
Wisconsin	1	No	None	1	90	15
Wyoming	1	No	None	1	90	No fee

Corporate Name

The first step your lawyer will take is to submit for approval by the state's corporation bureau one or more proposed corporate names in order to make certain that the name you choose is not already in use by an existing corporation. Hence, choosing a name (preferably two or three in case your first choice is disapproved) is your first order of business.

The corporation bureau will not check for duplication beyond the borders of its own state, and if you choose a name already in use by a large corporation, you run the risk of a lawsuit. But if, after checking in Standard and Poor's *Register of Corporations, Directors, and Executives*, you find that the name you want has not been pre-empted, you can proceed safely.

Aside from the prohibition against duplication, the only restriction on your choice of name is the requirement that the name include the word "corporation," "incorporated," or "limited" (or its abbreviation) so as to indicate to customers and creditors that they are, in fact, dealing with a corporation. This restriction aside, you can allow your imagination free range.

Your choice is likely to involve two basic decisions: whether to include your own name in the corporate name (David Jones, Inc.) and whether the name should suggest the corporation's principal business (Landscapers, Inc.). Some advisors caution against the use of your own name on the grounds that should the corporation fail, some personal stigma may persist. Overly specific names may prove a handicap if your corporation eventually includes or shifts to another type of business. The use of the word "associates" (as in David Smith Associates, Inc.) has become a cliché, but it owes its popularity to the fact that it is usefully vague and implies the existence of several key employees, even though it is often used by single-person corporations. In general, overly cute names should be avoided because they may date badly and may be meaningless or off-putting to some of your potential customers or clients.

Once the state's corporation bureau approves your corporate name, it will usually reserve it for your use for up to 60 days to give you time to file your certificate of incorporation.

Directors and Officers

Although the minimum number of directors and officers required for your corporation depends on the state in which you incorporate, the basic selection procedure for the closely held corporation is essentially the same everywhere. The shareholders – the people who capitalized the corporation and received its shares in return – elect a board of directors, and the board of directors elects officers: typically a president, vice president, treasurer, and secretary.

In the closely held corporation, any individual can fill any or all of these roles. If, for example, a husband and wife incorporate, it is common for them to share the outstanding stock between them (sometimes by owning it as joint tenants), for both of them to serve as the only directors, for one of them to serve as president and treasurer, and for the other to serve as vice president and secretary.

Sometimes, however, it may be necessary or useful to appoint additional people as directors or officers, especially if they can provide skills or knowledge that you and other incorporators lack. It is not necessary that any of these people be stockholders, but you may have to compensate them for their participation in directors' meetings or for any other duties. At least at the outset, you may find it easier to compensate these directors with stock, but giving them common stock involves some loss of control, and giving them preferred stock may require your corporation to pay them a dividend from profits on which the corporation pays taxes, whereas any cash fee you pay them is tax-deductible by the corporation.

Types and Number of Shares of Stock

Although the number, types, and par value of shares of stock to be issued by your corporation will depend on the laws of the state and the advice of your lawyer, you should have some understanding of the options open to you.

Common stock entitles each stockholder to exercise a vote at stockholders' meetings and to share whatever profits are declared as dividends, in proportion to the number of shares he or she owns. Because common stock is *voting* stock, it carries with it some control over all decisions made by the board of directors. Hence, if you decide to issue this kind of stock only, and if the question of control is important to you, you should make certain that you (alone or in conjunction with someone you trust) retain at least 51% of all the outstanding common stock.

Another way of dealing with the question of control is to draft the bylaws to authorize the issuance of two classes of stock: Class A, which enjoys both dividends and voting rights, and Class B, which receives dividends but has no voting rights. This procedure may be useful if you intend to take advantage of the estate-planning options that corporate structure offers (see p. 99).

Preferred stock guarantees its owners a specified dividend, which the corporation is required to pay before distributing any profits to its common stockholders. For example, an owner of Commonwealth Edison's preferred A stock must receive an annual dividend of $1.72 per share before any of the common stockholders may receive any dividends. Preferred stockholders have no voting rights unless the corporation fails to pay their dividends for a certain period. Since any stockholder may own both common and preferred stock and may, in fact, exchange one type for the other, the issuing of preferred stock can provide you with flexibility in distributing profits. The board of directors may decide, for example, to pay the dividend on preferred stock but to retain any excess profits as cash reserve, since they are under no obligation to pay dividends on common stock.

Regardless of the type or types of stock your corporation intends to issue, it is sometimes advisable to issue as few shares as possible and at the lowest possible par value (or no par value at all), since many state filing fees are based on these figures. Many closely held corporations start out with 100 shares of no-par-value stock. The par value of stock is almost meaningless; it reflects the total value of the corporation at the time the stock is issued. Thus, to issue 5,000 shares with a par value of $1.00, the corporation must have assets worth $5,000. But the real value of a share depends entirely on its actual worth in terms of the corporation's assets, liabilities, profits, and prospects.

Purpose of the Corporation

The laws of some states require that the purpose for which a corporation is established must be specified rather narrowly in the certificate of incorporation and that subsequent changes in the stated corporate purpose be approved by the state's corporation bureau. In other states, the stated purposes may be extremely broad. Your lawyer should strive for the maximum breadth and flexibility permitted by state law. A widely used phrase is "to engage in any lawful act or activity for which corporations may be organized."

As soon as your corporate name has been approved, your lawyer will prepare *articles of incorporation* (see Figure 8), which typically include the name and address of the corporation, a statement of its

Figure 8
ARTICLES OF INCORPORATION

C&S 500 (Rev. 8/93)

MICHIGAN DEPARTMENT OF COMMERCE - CORPORATION AND SECURITIES BUREAU

Date Received

(FOR BUREAU USE ONLY)

Name

Address

City   State   Zip Code

EFFECTIVE DATE

→ Document will be returned to the name and address you enter above ←

ARTICLES OF INCORPORATION
For use by Domestic Profit Corporations
(Please read information and instructions on the last page)

Pursuant to the provisions of Act 284, Public Acts of 1972, the undersigned corporation executes the following Articles:

ARTICLE I

The name of the corporation is:

ARTICLE II

The purpose or purposes for which the corporation is formed is to engage in any activity within the purposes for which corporations may be formed under the Business Corporation Act of Michigan.

ARTICLE III

The total authorized shares:

1. Common Shares _____

   Preferred Shares _____

2. A statement of all or any of the relative rights, preferences and limitations of the shares of each class is as follows:

purposes, the kinds and amounts of stock to be issued, the proposed term of the corporation, and the names and addresses of all incorporators. When these articles have been signed by all the incorporators, they will be submitted to the state's corporation bureau along with the required filing fee, which for a closely held corporation currently ranges from $20 to $300 (see Table 6).

Figure 8 (continued)
ARTICLES OF INCORPORATION

ARTICLE IV

1. The address of the registered office is:

_____ , Michigan _____
(Street Address)   (City)   (ZIP Code)

2. The mailing address of the registered office, if different than above:

_____ , Michigan _____
(Street Address or P.O. Box)   (City)   (ZIP Code)

3. The name of the resident agent at the registered office is: _____

ARTICLE V

The name(s) and address(es) of the incorporator(s) is (are) as follows:

Name   Residence or Business Address

_____

_____

_____

_____

_____

ARTICLE VI (Optional. Delete if not applicable)

When a compromise or arrangement or a plan of reorganization of this corporation is proposed between this corporation and its creditors or any class of them or between this corporation and its shareholders or any class of them, a court of equity jurisdiction within the state, on application of this corporation or of a creditor or shareholder thereof, or on application of a receiver appointed for the corporation, may order a meeting of the creditors or class of creditors or of the shareholders or class of shareholders to be affected by the proposed compromise or arrangement or reorganization, to be summoned in such manner as the court directs. If a majority in number representing 3/4 in value of the creditors or class of creditors, or of the shareholders or class of shareholders to be affected by the proposed compromise or arrangement or a reorganization, agree to a compromise or arrangement or a reorganization of this corporation as a consequence of the compromise or arrangement, the compromise or arrangement and the reorganization, if sanctioned by the court to which the application has been made, shall be binding on all the creditors or class of creditors, or on all the shareholders or class of shareholders and also on this corporation.

ARTICLE VII (Optional. Delete if not applicable)

Any action required or permitted by the Act to be taken at an annual or special meeting of shareholders may be taken without a meeting, without prior notice, and without a vote, if consents in writing, setting forth the action so taken, are signed by the holders of outstanding shares having not less than the minimum number of votes that would be necessary to authorize or take the action at a meeting at which all shares entitled to vote on the action were present and voted. The written consents shall bear the date of signature of each shareholder who signs the consent. No written consents shall be effective to take the corporate action referred to unless, within 60 days after the record date for determining shareholders entitled to express consent to or to dissent from a proposal without a meeting, written consents dated not more than 10 days before the record date and signed by a sufficient number of shareholders to take the action are delivered to the corporation. Delivery shall be to the corporation's registered office, its principal place of business, or an officer or agent of the corporation having custody of the minutes of the proceedings of its shareholders. Delivery made to a corporation's registered office shall be by hand or by certified or registered mail, return receipt requested.

Prompt notice of the taking of the corporate action without a meeting by less than unaminous written consent shall be given to shareholders who would have been entitled to notice of the shareholder meeting if the action had been taken at a meeting and who have not consented in writing.

If the corporation bureau approves the articles, you will be sent a *certificate of incorporation* (sometimes called the corporate *charter*), which is your corporation's formal authorization to get under way. In most states the corporation may begin conducting its business as soon as it receives its certificate, but some states require that an organizational meeting of the incorporators be held first.

Figure 8 (continued)
ARTICLES OF INCORPORATION

Use space below for additional Articles or for continuation of previous Articles. Please identify any Article being continued or added. Attach additional pages if needed.

I, (We), the incorporator(s) sign my (our) name(s) this _____ day of _____, 19_____ .

_____   _____

_____   _____

_____   _____

_____   _____

_____   _____

Once the certificate is in hand, the next step is to prepare the corporate *bylaws*, the set of rules that will govern the corporation's day-to-day operations. These bylaws usually specify the number of directors and officers the corporation will have, the scheduling of the annual meeting and the quorum of shareholders required to conduct business, the fiscal year to be used for tax purposes, the corporate

Figure 8 (continued)
ARTICLES OF INCORPORATION

C&S 500

Name of person or organization
remitting fees:

Preparer's name and business
telephone number:

(   )

INFORMATION AND INSTRUCTIONS

1. The articles of incorporation cannot be filed until this form, or a comparable document, is submitted.

2. Submit one original of this document. Upon filing, the document will be added to the records of the Corporation and Securities Bureau. The original will be returned to the address appearing in the box on the front as evidence of filing.

   Since this document will be maintained on optical disk media, it is important that the filing be legible. Documents with poor black and white contrast, or otherwise illegible, will be rejected.

3. This document is to be used pursuant to the provisions of Act 284, P.A. of 1972, by one or more persons for the purpose of forming a domestic profit corporation.

4. Article I - The corporate name of a domestic profit corporation is required to contain one of the following words or abbreviations: "Corporation", "Company", "Incorporated", "Limited", "Corp.", "Co.", "Inc.", or "Ltd.".

5. Article II - State, in general terms, the character of the particular business to be carried on. Under section 202(b) of the Act, it is sufficient to state substantially, alone or with specifically enumerated purposes, that the corporation may engage in any activity within the purposes for which corporations may be formed under the Act. The Act requires, however, that educational corporations state their specific purposes.

6. Article III - Indicate the total number of shares which the corporation has authority to issue. If there is more than one class or series of shares, state the relative rights, preferences and limitations of the shares of each class in Article III(2).

7. Article IV - A post office box may not be designated as the address of the registered office.

8. Article V - The Act requires one or more incorporators. Educational corporations are required to have at least three (3) incorporators. The address(es) should include a street number and name (or other designation), city and state.

9. The duration of the corporation should be stated in the articles only if the duration is not perpetual.

10. This document is effective on the date endorsed "filed" by the Bureau. A later effective date, no more than 90 days after the date of delivery, may be stated as an additional article.

11. The articles must be signed in ink by each incorporator. The names of the incorporators as set out in article V should correspond with the signatures.

12. **FEES:** Make remittance payable to the State of Michigan. Include corporation name on check or money order.

    NONREFUNDABLE FEE $10.00
    ORGANIZATION FEE: first 60,000 authorized shares or portion thereof $50.00
    TOTAL MINIMUM FEE $60.00
    ADDITIONAL ORGANIZATION FEE FOR AUTHORIZED SHARES OVER 60,000:
        each additional 20,000 authorized shares or portion thereof $30.00
        maximum fee for first 10,000,000 authorized shares $5,000.00
        each additional 20,000 authorized shares or portion thereof in excess of 10,000,000 shares $30.00
        maximum fee per filing for authorized shares in excess of 10,000,000 shares $200,000.00

13. Mail form and fee to:

    The office is located at:

    Michigan Department of Commerce
    Corporation and Securities Bureau
    Corporation Division
    P.O. Box 30054
    Lansing, MI 48909-7554

    6546 Mercantile Way
    Lansing, MI 48910
    Telephone: (517) 334-6302

policy on dividends, the bank to be used for corporate accounts, and the persons authorized to sign checks, contracts, and other documents on behalf of the corporation.

In large corporations, the bylaws are prepared by the initial incorporators and submitted to the shareholders for their approval. For a closely held corporation, however, your lawyer may provide you with a set of standard bylaws and adapt them in minor ways to accommodate the particular needs or circumstances of your business.

Once the bylaws have been prepared, the directors (who are usually all, but at least a majority, of the stockholders) can approve them on the spot. In such circumstances, the shareholders can, at this same meeting, elect directors and officers, authorize the issuance of stock certificates, and adopt resolutions concerning employment contracts and fringe benefits such as pension, profit-sharing, and health care plans, as well as other aspects of corporate operation.

Although we have noted the informality with which the directors' and stockholders' meetings of a closely held corporation can be conducted, the minutes of such meetings must be kept in considerable detail. To avoid possible future controversy among stockholders and with the IRS, the minutes should record the votes on every decision, along with a notation that a quorum was present. The same care should be exercised when the minutes are formally written up from the meeting notes, with a view to defending the corporation's existence against a possible challenge by the IRS that you are not using it as a bona fide business but are continuing to act as an individual under corporate guise.

USING YOUR CORPORATION FOR ESTATE PLANNING

The closely held corporation offers its shareholders, both during their lifetimes and after their deaths, opportunities for income tax reduction and for flexibility in estate planning not readily available from any other form of ownership.

Tax Reductions

One way to reduce your personal income tax is to give your children shares of stock. Because dividends on such stock are paid directly by the corporation to the children, they are taxable to the children, presumably at a much lower rate than yours. If the children have reached the age of majority, they can use these dividends for any purpose they choose. If they are minors, their dividends can be used for such "extra" expenses as summer camp, orthodontia, or college tuition. If they are under age 14, any unearned income in excess of $1,200 will be subject to the "kiddie tax" discussed on page 83.

Figure 9
MINUTES OF FIRST MEETING OF BOARD OF DIRECTORS

The first meeting of the Board of Directors of XYZ Corporation was held at 101 Miller St., Lansing, Michigan, on the 1st day of July, 1995 at 7:00 PM.

The following, representing a quorum of all the directors, were present: John Doe and Mary Doe.

A motion was made, seconded and carried that John Doe be elected temporary chairman and that Mary Doe be elected temporary secretary.

After being nominated, the following were unanimously elected to serve as officers of the corporation for one (1) year:

President and Vice President: John Doe
Secretary and Treasurer: Mary Doe

A motion was made, seconded and carried that the seal proposed by the secretary, identical to the impression made on these minutes, be adopted as the oficial seal of the corporation.

Upon motions made, seconded and carried, it was

RESOLVED, that the president and treasurer be authorized to issue, as certificates for shares of the corporation, the certificates shown to this meeting, copies of which are appended to these minutes;

RESOLVED, that the share and transfer book presented to this meeting be adopted as the share and transfer book of the corporation;

RESOLVED, that the treasurer be authorized to open a checking account for purposes of deposits and withdrawals in the name of the corporation at the First Bank of Lansing, Lansing, Michigan, and that withdrawals from such account be made only by John Doe or Mary Doe.

The secretary then presented a proposal to the corporation from John Doe, to transfer the assets of Doe's Distributing, of which he is the owner, to the corporation as of the 1st day of July, 1995. In consideration of such transfer, subject to all outstanding liabilities, John Doe proposes to receive 100 shares of the common stock of the corporation.

The proposal was considered by the Board. A motion was made, seconded and carried that the proposal was accepted.

RESOLVED, that the offer, as set forth in the above proposal, represents a fair offer to the corporation and should therefore be and is hereby accepted.

RESOLVED, that the president and treasurer of the corporation be authorized to accept delivery of the assets and to issue to John Doe, in full payment thereof, 100 fully paid shares of the common stock of the corporation.

There being no further business, a motion was made, seconded and carried that the meeting be adjourned. Dated the 1st day of July, 1995.

_____
Mary Doe, Secretary-Treasurer

Appended hereto:
Corporate Seal
Copies of Stock Certificates

There are two possible pitfalls in such a plan. First, if the value of the stock plus any other gifts you make to each child in any one year exceeds $10,000 (or $20,000 with the consent of your spouse), you may be subject to federal gift tax (see Chap. 2). But making annual gifts below these limits can avoid this problem.

A second problem may arise from the fact that any dividends paid on your children's shares must also be paid on your own shares, which may have the effect of increasing your own income tax. But this can be avoided in two ways. First, you can give your children only preferred stock (on which dividends *must* be paid) and retain for yourself the common stock (on which dividends need be paid only at the discretion of the directors). Alternatively, your corporation can have two classes of common stock: 10 percent Class A, which has voting rights, and 90 percent Class B, which does not. If you give your children all the Class B stock, they will receive 90 percent of the dividends and you will receive only 10 percent, but you will retain full control of the corporation, perhaps eventually passing on your Class A stock to the child whom you regard as most able and willing to continue the corporation after your death.

If, on the other hand, you would like to relinquish control of your corporation but not the income, you can give a child or some other beneficiary the common stock and retain the preferred stock, which assures you of a continuing income as long as the corporation is profitable. Should the corporation fail to pay dividends on its preferred stock for a certain length of time, you, as a preferred stockholder, can gain voting rights and make changes in the management.

Planning for Your Beneficiaries

One of the major advantages of a corporation is its immortality. On your death, the corporation can continue without interruption provided only that you have authorized another corporate officer (your spouse or an adult child, for example) to carry on the business. Other than your individually owned shares, nothing in the corporation is involved in the probate administration of your estate.

Of course, your corporate stock, like any other assets, can be placed in whatever form of ownership promises to avoid probate: joint tenancy, tenancy by the entirety, or a revocable or irrevocable living trust. In all these forms of ownership, you can retain control of the corporation if you retain 51 percent of the voting stock or if you can obtain the proxies of your joint tenant or the trustee of any trust-owned stock.

One significant advantage of the corporate form of ownership is that it enables you to divide corporate assets rather precisely among your beneficiaries. You can, for example, give 30 percent of your stock to each of your three children and 5 percent to each of two nieces. This would be extremely impracticable if you were operating as a sole proprietorship or a partnership.

In addition, by adopting a long-term program of giving shares of stock to your children or grandchildren, you can conveniently pass on to them the ownership of a business or a family farm. Making periodic gifts of shares is far more effective than, for example, attempting to transfer title to 100 acres worth $500,000 by dividing it into $10,000 two-acre parcels and transferring them piecemeal.

Further, if you include in your employment contract with the corporation a death benefit clause for payments not exceeding $5,000 per employee, this money will, under current law, pass to your beneficiaries without being subject to estate tax or to federal income tax.

WITHDRAWING FROM YOUR CORPORATION

Although your corporation is legally immortal, there may come a time—your retirement, for example—when you would like either to withdraw from it or to dissolve it altogether. Either decision is fairly simple to carry out.

If you decide to withdraw, you simply sell your shares either to the corporation itself or to one or more fellow shareholders. The formula for determining share value should have been embodied in a stock purchase agreement executed when you incorporated, but in its absence an outside professional appraiser can be used. For tax purposes, any sale of your stock is treated as a capital gain or loss.

If, on the other hand, you and the other stockholders decide to dissolve the corporation, each of you may turn in your stock to the corporation and receive in exchange your proportional share of the corporation's assets. These assets need not be in cash. If, for example, you and your spouse own 100 percent of the stock and the corporation's assets include an automobile, a computer, and 500 shares of Commonwealth Edison common stock, you can have the corporation sell some or all of these items and pay you in cash or, if you prefer, you can take these items at fair market value in exchange for your stock. In either case, the transaction is subject to tax as a capital gain or capital loss.

Even though capital gains are taxed at only 28%, liquidating your corporation, especially if it has accumulated substantial assets, can burden you with a heavy income tax liability. You can, however, reduce the tax consequences by liquidating the corporation piecemeal over a period of time and thus spread the capital gain instead of taking it all in one year.

An Alternative to the Corporation

The most important recent development in the choice of ways to own a business has been the rapidly increasing use of the limited liability company (LLC), a first cousin to the traditional corporation. An LLC, which is formed pursuant to a state enabling statute, is a form of ownership that provides insulation from liability to the same extent as a corporation; is treated as a partnership for tax purposes; and provides its owners with the option of personally managing the business or designating owners or nonowners as managers. The combination of the corporate characteristic of limited liability with favorable passthrough tax treatment (like partnerships and S corporations) has encouraged the enactment of state LLC laws in recent years. As of this writing, 40 states have passed laws permitting use of the LLC.

Prior to the emergence of LLCs, taxpayers seeking to combine limited liability with passthrough tax treatment were limited to the use of the S corporation. LLCs afford more flexibility than S corporations in several respects, including the following:

Unlike S corporations, which may have no more than 35 shareholders, an LLC may have an unlimited number of members.

While only individuals, estates, and certain trusts may be shareholders of S corporations, LLCs normally may include corporations, partnerships, trusts, and other entities as members.

The one-class-of-stock requirement, which may impose a burden on S corporations, does not apply to an LLC.

An LLC enjoys other tax advantages not available to an S corporation.

The primary advantage of an LLC over a partnership is the lack of personal liability of its owners. In addition, LLCs provide more flexibility in management of a business than do partnerships.

A Postscript

If you have read this chapter carefully, the likelihood is that you see some strong advantages to incorporation and that you are undaunted by the responsibilities and routines we have described. If this is the case, we invite you to go ahead. Because so many people see incorporation as an almost magical and cost-free financial panacea, we have perhaps overemphasized its limitations and its pitfalls, neglecting to stress that many thousands of people in every part of the country find the closely held corporation the most efficient form of ownership for many of their assets.

CHAPTER 6

ASSETS THAT NEED SPECIAL CONSIDERATION

In Chapters 2 through 5, we were primarily concerned with explaining the advantages and limitations of the various forms of ownership for the kinds of property most commonly owned by the typical middle-income individual or family. For the sake of clarity, we were forced to generalize to some extent and to ignore for the time being certain kinds of property whose ownership requires special consideration and, hence, more extended discussion. The purpose of this chapter is to provide more detailed information and advice concerning certain assets that may require special management or that may present problems if you simply assume that they should be held in the same form of ownership as all your other assets.

Unlike the preceding chapters, this chapter need not be read from beginning to end. A skimming of the section headings or a search in the index will identify those types of assets that are of interest to you, either because you own them or because you plan to acquire them.

PERSONAL PROPERTY

Everything you own is legally classified as either real property or personal property. Real property, such as land and buildings, is immovable. Its ownership is invariably documented in the form of a deed or land contract and usually recorded with a government agency, typically the county register of deeds. Personal property, such as motor vehicles, bank accounts, household furnishings, and personal effects, is movable, and its ownership may or may not be documented or registered. Ownership of your automobile, for example, is documented by its certificate of title and registered with the state department of motor vehicles. Ownership of your bank account is documented by your passbook, your certificate of deposit, or a bank's signature card. Most items of your personal property, however, are probably undocumented, especially if you have owned them for a number of years. Some may originally have had documentation in the form of a bill of sale or receipt; others, such as the lawnmower you bought at a garage sale, or the Roman coin given to you by a friend, have no documentation whatever, even though they may have considerable value.

During your lifetime, the absence of documentation for most items of personal property is likely to be unimportant unless you must file an insurance claim for their loss or destruction—in which case photographs can serve as useful substitutes for (or supplements to) ownership documents. In general, your ownership of the oil painting over your fireplace is not likely to be challenged, and if you attempt to sell your expensive camera through a classified advertisement, the buyer is unlikely to demand written proof that you own it.

On your death, however, questions may arise either in connection with probate or as a result of disputes among your survivors. Even in the absence of documentation, your household furnishings and equipment will be assumed to have been owned jointly with your spouse, and he or she will assume ownership of them automatically. But does this apply also to your stamp collection, which you always intended to leave to your younger son, or to the garden tractor you bought in an informal partnership with a neighbor, or to the unregistered bond found in your bank safe deposit box? In the absence of any documentation, such items will be presumed to belong to you alone and hence will be subject both to probate and, if your estate is substantial, to federal and state death taxes.

Undocumented personal property can become a source of contention among your survivors. Will your surviving spouse sell your favorite shotgun to a dealer despite your son's claim that you orally promised it to him? Or, if you become a widower, are your three daughters likely to quarrel among themselves or with you over ownership of your wife's jewelry or her Haviland china?

To some extent these problems can be circumvented by a properly drawn will, but no will should or can account for every one of the valuable possessions that you may possess at the time of your death. A simpler solution is to document the ownership of each of these items by a written statement.

If, for example, you intend your younger son to inherit your stamp collection, a signed and dated statement explicitly placing it into joint tenancy between you and him will ensure that your intention will be carried out. If you want your elder daughter to have your Haviland collection and your younger one to have your jewelry, similar written acknowledgments of joint tenancy will suffice. (See Figure 3.)

As for the unregistered bond and other untitled valuables in your safe deposit box, a written statement specifying their ownership should be attached to each of them. And to avoid misunderstandings in connection with the garden-tractor partnership, a statement can be prepared and signed by you and your neighbor indicating that the ownership is a tenancy in common, which means that each of you owns an equal share and that no automatic inheritance is intended upon the death of either of you.

MOTOR VEHICLES

The document evidencing your ownership of a motor vehicle is its certificate of title. In some states this is combined with its certificate of registration, but in others it is a separate document. The registration certificate should always be carried in the vehicle or by its driver. The title should be kept in a safe place, because neither you nor your survivors can sell or transfer the vehicle without it.

The name in which a vehicle is registered needs careful consideration, because most states hold the owner as well as the driver responsible for damages resulting from its negligent operation. Hence, if an auto accident damage claim results in a settlement or judgment that exceeds the liability insurance covering the vehicle, the owner's other assets may be attached. This is not a uncommon event, because juries often award six-figure damages against owners who carry only the $30,000–$50,000 minimum liability insurance coverages required by some states.

Thus, if most of your assets are held in tenancy by the entirety, your automobile should be registered in your individual name. In this way, only your individual assets will be vulnerable in case of a catastrophic accident and the jointly held assets will be fully insulated from creditors' claims. If a married couple owns two vehicles, each of the spouses should register in his or her name the one he or she drives most the time.

Some couples register their vehicles jointly in order to avoid probate, but this precaution is unnecessary because almost all states provide a simple procedure for the after-death transfer of motor vehicle titles to a surviving family member without the need for probate. If the survivor presents the vehicle title and an affidavit of heirship, the state motor vehicle department will, for a nominal fee, issues a new title in his or her name.

If you have a teenaged son, you may be tempted to register his vehicle in your name in the hope that the multiple-vehicle discount offered by your insurance company will offset the very high premiums charged young male drivers. But these high premiums reflect the very high accident rate for teenaged males, and hence, unless you carry very high liability coverage, registering his vehicle in your name may be risky if your solely owned assets are worth more than his and he is found liable for an accident involving serious injury or death.

If you are involved in a closely held corporation and use a vehicle for business purposes, registering it in the name of the corporation allows the corporation to pay (and tax-deduct) not only all operating insurance, and maintenance costs but also its depreciation. However, the corporation will also be exposed to liability for auto accident damage claims in excess of liability insurance coverage. A better alternative may be for you to register the vehicle in your own name and either tax-deduct its operating costs as an employment-related expense or have the corporation reimburse you for its use on a per-mile basis.

BANK ACCOUNTS

Bank accounts may be registered in any of the forms of ownership described in Chapters 2 through 5, but two problems may arise in connection with joint ownership accounts because of their provision for automatic inheritance by the survivor.

First, many joint accounts that are established solely for the sake of convenience result in unintended inheritance. For example, an elderly mother of several children may establish a joint account with one of her sons simply to enable him to pay her bills and manage her finances generally. On her death, however, he will automatically acquire the existing account balance and the other children will be excluded. This situation can be avoided by a written statement, signed and dated by both the mother and the son, specifying that the account was titled jointly for convenience only and that neither party intended that the entire account balance belong to the son on the mother's death. Alternatively, the mother could retain the account in her name alone and give the son her power of attorney (see Chap. 2) authorizing him to manage it, or she could transfer the account to a revocable living trust with herself as trustee and the son as successor or co-trustee.

A related problem—one that sometimes results in litigation—arises when one of the joint tenants inadvertently wills funds held in a joint account to someone other than the joint tenant. Jointly held property cannot effectively be willed by one of the joint tenants if any other tenant survives. Hence, it is often desirable, though not absolutely necessary, for each joint tenant to specify in his will or some other written statement that he both understands and intends that the surviving tenant will automatically be entitled to the bank account balance and that it therefore is not to be included in his probate estate.

REAL ESTATE
(SEE ALSO CONDOMINIUMS AND COOPERATIVES)

Real estate, both residential and commercial, can be held in any of the forms of ownership described in Chapters 2 through 5. There are, however, one or two restrictions. Minors, although they may hold real estate, may neither buy nor sell it except through a guardian or conservator. Many states permit aliens to own property but some limit its amount or the length of time they may own it; others completely prohibit aliens from owning real estate.

Ownership Rights and Restrictions

Ownership of a piece of real property includes *mineral rights*—that is, ownership of everything below the surface of the ground—unless these rights have been explicitly reserved or excepted by the seller.

This means that if oil, coal, or other mineral deposits are discovered in the vicinity, you can lease to an individual or a company the right to explore for and extract the minerals, usually on a royalty basis. If you sell the property, you may be able to reserve all or part of the mineral rights and continue to receive royalties.

Your *air rights*—ownership of the airspace over and around your property—are somewhat more limited. You are entitled to ownership of the airspace that you can in some way reasonably use or enjoy, and this right protects you against neighbors' trees or structures that overhang or intrude on your property. You cannot, however, prevent aircraft from flying over your property unless you can prove that such flights interfere with your use of the property—for example, if low-flying planes frighten your dairy cows and lower their milk production.

Like your ownership of guns and motor vehicles, your ownership of real estate is not absolute; you cannot do what you please with it. Instead, your use of the property is invariably restricted by agencies of state and local government and, not infrequently, by private parties as well.

Governmental restrictions most commonly take the form of zoning ordinances, building codes, environmental laws, fire and other safety codes, and similar laws, which regulate both the construction and equipment of buildings and the uses to which they and the land may be put. The police power of the local government may, for example, prevent you from (or punish you for) installing a water heater by yourself, building a storage shed behind your house, dredging a wetland, dealing with business clients at your home, operating garage sales on a regular basis, or even allowing your lawn to become unkempt.

In addition, under its right of *eminent domain,* the government can condemn your property if the land is proven essential for some public purpose: a reservoir, for example, or a highway or a public hospital. The government is, of course, obligated to pay you fair market value for your condemned property, a figure that will be determined by a court, and sometimes a jury, if you and the governmental agency cannot agree on a purchase price.

The taxing power of government constitutes perhaps the most stringent limitation on your ownership of real property, because delinquency in paying real estate taxes has more immediate consequences than delinquency in the payment of other bills. If you become delinquent on even the most trivial real estate tax, the government has the right, without court action, to force the sale of your property to collect the tax.

Your property rights may also be affected by certain *easements*, such as the right of access to part of your property by utility companies to make repairs to their lines or to prune trees that threaten to interfere with overhead wires, or the right of water companies to repair drains or sewers that cross or abut your property.

Shorefront property is subject to special limitations. If your property abuts a body of tidal water, your ownership extends only to the high-tide mark, and the land between the high- and low-tide marks is open to use by the public. If your property abuts a nonnavigable stream or lake, the property is considered to extend to its center. But if the body of water on which your property fronts is navigable, then the public has the right to use any part of the water, although it may not trespass on your property to gain access to it.

Private restraints on your ownership rights generally take the form of "restrictive covenants," often formulated by a real-estate developer who has subdivided a large area for sale to individual homeowners. In order to preserve what he perceives to be the character of the neighborhood, the developer may establish a set of regulations covering such matters as minimum cost, size, and set-back of buildings, the display of signs, the erection of fences, the parking of recreational or commercial vehicles, and similar matters. Purchasers of land in such developments are required to comply with these restrictions.

Whether all restrictive covenants are enforceable is not altogether clear. Several decades ago, when covenants barring the sale of homes to members of minority groups were challenged on the grounds that they violated the civil rights of such groups, the U.S. Supreme Court decided that these covenants were not illegal because they had not been imposed by a governmental unit, but that they were unenforceable because their enforcement by a court would constitute government participation in the violation of a group's civil rights.

As a result, restrictive covenants barring minority racial and ethnic groups have disappeared, but the validity of other restrictive covenants is uncertain. Violating a restrictve covenant is not a criminal offense. Hence, if you were to violate a restriction, one or more of your neighbors would have to bring suit against you for injunctive relief—an eventuality that is rather unlikely unless your violation is grossly offensive.

Real vs. Personal Property

When real estate is bought or sold, the distinction between real and personal property becomes important because, unless the buyer and seller stipulate otherwise, the purchase agreement applies to real property only and not to personal property.

Generally speaking, anything permanently affixed to the property is regarded as real property, whereas anything that is removable without damage to the building is regarded as personal property. Thus, a portable dishwasher is personal property and is not automatically included in the transaction, whereas a built-in model goes with the house. Because the status of traverse rods, chandeliers, automatic garage-door openers, Franklin-type fireplaces, bird baths, garden plantings, and similar items is often ambiguous, they should be specified clearly in any real estate sales agreement.

Documentation of Ownership

Just as your purchase of a valuable piece of personal property is evidenced by a receipt or a bill of sale, so your purchase of real property is evidenced by a deed or a land contract describing the property and signed by the seller. Even if the seller owned the property as an individual, you should, as purchaser, insist that both the seller and his spouse sign the deed, because in some states the seller's spouse may retain "dower" or "curtesy" rights to the property, which, without his or her signature, prevent your receiving a clear title.

Unlike a bill of sale or an assignment of personal property, a real estate deed should be promptly recorded in the office of the register of deeds in the county in which the property is situated. Until your deed has been recorded, there is nothing to prevent the person who sold it to you from subsequently selling it to another person and issuing him a deed. If this second purchaser is without actual notice of your purchase and records his deed before you do, your rights to the property will be lost.

If you inherit property through a will, no deed is involved. Instead, as evidence of your ownership and your right to sell or mortgage the property, you should record with the local register of deeds a copy of the will along with a copy of the order of the probate court assigning the property to you.

If property belongs to someone who dies without a will, the probate court will decide which of the owner's survivors are entitled under state law to what share of it and will issue an order assigning the respective portions of the deceased's interest to them.

Mortgages vs. Land Contracts

The purchase of real estate can be financed either through a mortgage or in some states through a land contract. The differences between these two instruments are worth noting.

Under a mortgage, title to the property passes to the purchaser (the mortgagor), who buys it with money lent him by the mortgagee – either an individual, a lending institution, or the seller of the property. To obtain this loan the purchaser signs (1) a promissory note, which specifies the principal to be paid, the schedule of payments, and the interest rate, and (2) a mortgage or, in some states, a deed of trust, which pledges the property as collateral for the loan.

If the buyer defaults on his mortgage payments or fails to pay taxes or insurance premiums on the property, the mortgagee has the right, subject to state law, to foreclose on the mortgage – that is, to force a public sale of the property in order to recoup the unpaid balance of his loan. If the sale proceeds are less than the amount of the loan, the mortgagee can apply to the court for a "deficiency judgment," which requires the mortgagor to make up the deficit. If, on the other hand, the sale proceeds exceed the loan balance, the excess, less the expenses incurred in the foreclosure proceedings and any other liens on the property, is payable to the defaulting mortgagor.

To protect mortgagors in the event of foreclosure, the laws of many states permit the mortgagor a certain period of time – usually up to one year – within which to "redeem" or buy back the property at the foreclosure price plus interest and foreclosure costs. This right of redemption is especially useful if the property is sold at a foreclosure price far below its actual value.

A land contract, which is not available in all states, differs from a mortgage in that it does not immediately transfer legal title of the property to the purchaser. Instead, it is a contract between seller and buyer in which the seller promises to sell and the buyer promises to buy a piece of property at a specified price and on a specified payment schedule. The contract gives the purchaser immediate possession of the property, but actual legal title to the property is not transferred until the purchaser has completed his schedule of payments. In the interim, the purchaser assumes responsibility for paying all taxes and insurance premiums and for maintaining the property in good repair.

In case of default on a land contract, the foreclosure procedure and the defaulting purchaser's redemption rights are essentially the same as those governing a mortgage, with one significant exception. The foreclosure of a land contract that is in default invariably requires the lender to file a lawsuit and obtain a judgment from a court before the foreclosure sale can take place—often a time-consuming and expensive procedure. Foreclosing a mortgage that contains a "power of sale" clause does not require a lawsuit in advance of the mortgage sale. The mortgagees need merely advertise in a local newspaper that the sale will take place, give written notice to the mortgagor, and then proceed with it. In this respect, a mortgage is preferable from the lender's point of view, a land contract preferable from the purchaser's perspective.

LIFE INSURANCE POLICIES

The proceeds of your life insurance policies are not probate assets if they are paid to beneficiaries other than your estate or your personal representative. But if, as is almost invariably the case, you are the owner of the policies, the proceeds will be included as part of your estate for the assessment of possible federal estate tax. You can avoid exposing the proceeds to estate tax, however, by transferring ownership of the policies to someone else—presumably the primary beneficiary or, in some circumstances, to an irrevocable trust.

Transferring ownership of a life insurance policy requires nothing more than executing an assignment form (available from your agent or from the insurance company's home office) and delivering it to the company. But because the transfer is irrevocable, you need to recognize that by making it you give up forever the right to change beneficiaries, surrender the policy for cash, borrow on it, or use it as collateral for a loan. Moreover, you are transferring to the new owner both the responsibility for future premium payments and the right to change the beneficiaries you originally designated.

Because the assignment of a policy is considered a gift, it will be subject to federal gift tax if the cash surrender value of the policy at the time of the assignment exceeds $10,000 (or $20,000 with a spouse's consent). If the total cash surrender value of two or more policies exceeds this amount, you may be able to avoid this exposure to gift tax by assigning each of them in a different calendar year or to a different person. Bear in mind, however, that term insurance policies have no cash surrender value at any time and therefore may be assigned without gift tax liability.

Whether or not you assign your life insurance policies, you need to consider your designation of beneficiaries carefully and monitor the situation regularly. If one of your designated beneficiaries is a minor or an incompetent adult, it may be preferable to designate as beneficiary a trust of some sort (see Chap. 4) instead of the guardian (see Chap. 7). Furthermore, if all your designated beneficiaries predecease you, the proceeds will go to your estate by default, even if you have assigned the policy to another person.

SECURITIES

Securities—stocks, bonds, and various government instruments—can be held in any type of ownership, but if they are intended for a minor they should be registered in a custodial account (see Chap. 4), because a minor cannot legally buy or sell them. Whatever their ownership, they can be held by you in the form of actual certificates or kept in your account by your broker. There are advantages and disadvantages to each alternative.

Holding the Certificates

If you hold the certificates yourself, you receive the dividends promptly (or you can direct the corporation paying the dividends to deposit them directly into your bank or money market account) and thus begin earning interest on them at the earliest possible date. In addition, you can sell them through any broker you choose and not necessarily through the one from whom you bought them. Lastly, if the shares are owned jointly and held in the form of registered certificates, your tax liability is shared with the joint owner, regardless of which of you actually paid for the shares. If such jointly owned shares are held in the broker's "street name," the tax liability is governed by state law, which should be consulted.

On the other hand, holding the certificates yourself risks their theft or loss or involves the (tax-deductible) rental of a safe deposit box. Moreover, if you decide to transfer them or sell them through a new broker, the signatures of all owners must appear on the back of each certificate and must be guaranteed by a bank or a brokerage firm. This can create a problem if one of the owners is not available when the signatures are required, and an even greater problem if one of the owners dies. By contrast, if the securities are held by your broker, a single telephone call can accomplish almost any transaction.

If you decide to hold the certificates yourself, you should make sure to retain also the broker's transaction slip as proof of your ownership and as a tax record to document gains or losses.

Changing the ownership of a stock certificate (as distinct from selling it) does not require the services of a broker or the payment of a commission. All you need do is execute and sign the reverse of the certificate, have the signature(s) guaranteed by your bank, and send the certificate to the corporation's transfer agent, whose address can be obtained from the shareholder relations department of the issuing corporation.

Leaving the Securities with Your Broker

If you leave the securities in your brokerage account, they will not be registered in your name but will be titled in what is called the broker's "street name" account. There is virtually no risk of loss in case the brokerage firm should go bankrupt, because most brokers are members of Securities Investors' Protection Corp. (SIPC), which insures your account in much the same way that the Federal Deposit Insurance Corp. (FDIC) insures your bank account.

Keeping your securities in your broker's account not only relieves you of responsibility for their safekeeping but also simplifies your income tax chores, because most brokers provide their customers with end-of-year statements of dividends and interest received. Selling your securities, especially if they are jointly owned, is also simplified because it requires only a telephone call from one of the owners instead of the guaranteed signatures of both. (Whether you regard this as a convenience or a risk depends on your relationship with your joint tenant.) If you are an active trader, leaving your securities certificates with the broker can avoid countless trips to your safe deposit box, to your bank, and to the post office.

All these services, however, are not without some cost. Although most stock dividends are payable on the first or the fifteenth of the month, brokers customarily accumulate them and transmit them to customers at the end of each month, retaining for themselves the fifteen or thirty days' interest. This may be insignificant if your dividends amount to only $100 or so each month, but if you own bonds that pay semiannual interest of $1,000 or more on the first of the month, your loss of a month's interest twice a year may strike you as a high price to pay for the convenience of a broker's street account.

SAFE DEPOSIT BOXES

The decision as to whether to rent a safe deposit box as an individual or jointly with another person or persons hinges on two issues: (1) access to it, both during life and after death and (2) determining the ownership of its contents. Figure 10 is an example of a safe deposit box lease.

Accessibility

The individual who rents a safe deposit box in his own name alone may have difficulty in retrieving its contents if they are needed unexpectedly—when, for example, he suddenly needs to sell his gold coins, or when a bond that he owns is called—and he is for any reason unable to get to the bank. This problem can easily be solved by giving a friend or relative the key along with a power of attorney (see Chap. 2) authorizing one-time or long-term access to the box, but in fact this is done infrequently because most people do not foresee such contingencies.

When the bank is notified of the death of an individual renter, the box becomes inaccessible to anyone except his court-appointed personal representative. In most states, however, survivors can obtain a probate court order giving them access to the box for the limited purpose of retrieving a will or a deed to a cemetery lot, with the understanding that the will is to be deposited immediately with the probate court. In many states, the personal representative may not remove any of the contents unless a representative of the state treasurer is present to inventory its contents for tax purposes.

Usually the bank can summon a treasury representative within a matter of hours, but occasionally the delay can cause problems—when, for example, the box contains instructions for funeral rites or anatomical gifts and these are not retrieved in time to be complied with.

The problem of lifetime access is less likely to arise when a box is rented jointly with a spouse, child, or friend, because such a box is normally accessible to any co-renter, and each co-renter is provided

Figure 10
SAFE DEPOSIT BOX LEASE

SAFE DEPOSIT BOX LEASE

First of America Bank-Central
PO Box 30120, Lansing, Michigan 48909

BOX NO._____

RENTAL $_____
(DUE ANNUALLY IN ADVANCE)

The **First of America Bank-Central**, in consideration of the foregoing rental, the receipt of one annual installment of which is hereby acknowledged, hereby leases unto the undersigned Lessee its safe deposit box bearing the above number, in its Safe Deposit Vault, for a period of one year from the date hereof, and thereafter in subsequent terms of one year each, upon the same terms, as are herein contained, until this lease be terminated in a manner hereinafter provided.

1. The Bank shall not be considered a bailee or otherwise in control or possession of the contents of the leased box, the relation of the Bank and Lessee, under this agreement, being that solely of landlord and tenant.

2. The Bank will retain no keys which will open any leased box, and the keys thereto must be returned upon the surrender of said box. Any expense incurred by the Bank, occasioned by the loss of a key or by failure to deliver the same at the time of cancellation or surrender, shall be paid by the Lessee. Lessee must notify the Bank at once if a key is lost.

3. The Bank may comply with all orders of any court relative to such box and shall not be liable to Lessee for any loss or damage resulting therefrom.

4. Papers must not be examined within the vault; suitable rooms are provided for that purpose. Lessee himself must remove and replace the box. Neither the Bank nor any officer or employee thereof, shall be authorized to act as deputy or agent for the Lessee in respect to said box. Should an attendant handle the box as an accommodation to the Lessee, the Bank assumes no liability therfor.

5. Lessee shall have access to the box only during hours when the Bank is open for business and for such additional times, if any, as the Bank may prescribe.

6. Lessee shall give the Bank the signature of each person authorized to have access to such box and such signature shall, until written revocation be filed with the Bank, be conclusive evidence of his assent to the terms hereof; identification by signature shall be sufficient. In case of death, insolvency or other legal disability of Lessee, access may be granted to Lessee's legal representative, after such notice as may be required by law has been given to the county treasurer or other public official.

7. The duty of the Bank in respect to property deposited in said box is limited to ordinary care in the performance of their duties by employees and officers of the Bank. An unauthorized opening shall not be presumed or inferred from partial or total loss of contents.

8. All rentals shall be payable in advance and the Bank may refuse access to the box until all charges therefor have been paid. In the event of non-payment the Bank shall have such remedies as are or may be provided by state law.

9. The Bank shall not be liable for any delay caused by failure of the vault doors or locks to operate. Lessee shall not use said box or permit the same to be used, for the deposit of any intoxicating liquors, narcotics or any property of an explosive or destructive nature.

10. This contract is personal to the Lessee and shall not be assigned or transferred, and any assignment or transfer thereof shall immediately terminate it. Lessee hereby acknowledges the receipt of two keys to said box and a duplicate of this lease.

11. The Bank shall be immediately notified in writing of any change of address of Lessee, and in the absence of any written notice to the Bank of a change, a notice mailed to the address given by Lessee at the time of making this contract shall be sufficient for all purposes.

12. If this lease is with two or more persons, their rights therein shall be as described by state law. If Lessee is a corporation, its officers or agents authorized to have access to such box at the date of this lease shall be presumed to have like authority thereafter until due written notice of a change therein is received by the Bank.

13. The Bank reserves the right to cancel any lease after ten days' notice by mail to the address of Lessee on its records and the return of the unearned rental for the unexpired term of the lease.

14. The Bank reserves the right to make such other and further reasonable rules and regulations, without notice, as it may from time to time consider needful for the safety, care and cleanliness of the premises and for the preservation of good order therein.

Dated at Lansing, Michigan_____19_____

First of America Bank-Central

By_____
Manager, Safe Deposit Department

_____
Lessee

_____
Lessee

Address_____Street

City_____State_____

with a key. Hence any contents urgently needed by one of the renters can, in his absence, be retrieved by the other.

Under such an arrangement, of course, the co-renters must have a stable relationship and enjoy complete trust in one another, because there is nothing to prevent one of them from opening the box at any time and absconding with negotiable items such as cash or unregistered bonds. But most people who trust one another sufficiently to have established joint ownership of a house or securities are likely to be joint renters of the box in which the deeds or the stock certificates are stored.

This flexibility of access, however, may (and usually will) be terminated by the bank immediately on the death of any one of the joint renters. As soon as it is notified of the death, the bank in some states is required by law to seal the box until a representative of the state treasury arrives. As in the case of the individually owned box, however, the survivors can obtain a court order authorizing access to search for and retrieve a will or a cemetery deed.

When a joint renter dies but the bank has not yet been notified, it is perfectly legal for the surviving renter to get access to the box, remove its contents, and place them in another box, rented in his or her own name, thus avoiding delay as well as any inventory by the state treasurer's representative.

Establishing Ownership

The inventory of the contents of a safe deposit box for tax purposes usually presents less of a problem than establishing the ownership of some of the contents, not merely for death-tax appraisal but also for determining the need for probate administration.

Whether the box is rented individually or by co-renters, no problem will arise in connection with contents whose ownership is clearly documented—with the deed for a jointly owned house, for example, or with securities registered under individual or joint ownership. On the other hand, contents whose ownership is not documented—such things as unregistered bonds, cash, stamp collections, diamonds, and bullion—may be regarded as the property of the deceased tenant even if the box was rented jointly. Women's jewelry is likely to be regarded as the wife's property if it is stored in a box jointly rented by spouses, but questions as to its ownership are likely to arise if the box is co-rented by two brothers.

There are two ways to avoid this problem. First, it is possible to attach to each of the unregistered contents either its original bill of sale or a signed statement specifying its ownership (see Figure 4). An alternative, of use primarily to married couples, is for each spouse to rent a box individually and to store in it everything (including the will) that belongs to the *other* spouse. On the death of either spouse, only his or her box will be sealed, and when the contents are inventoried the state representative will find nothing that is taxable to the renter. Either spouse can have access to the other's box at any time if each of them executes a power of attorney for this purpose.

Regardless of whether a box is rented individually or jointly, its rental is tax-deductible if it is used for the safekeeping of any contents that produce or are expected to produce income—stock certificates, gold, leases, contracts, and the like.

IRA AND KEOGH ACCOUNTS

Individual Retirement Accounts (IRAs) and Keogh Accounts are tax-sheltered individual pension plans. Anyone who is not covered by another retirement plan and whose income does not exceed certain limits can open an IRA and deposit into it a maximum of $2,000 of earned income annually. The Keogh plan, which has higher contribution limits, is available only for self-employment income—earnings from full- or part-time work, which are not employee wages.

In either plan the contributions are tax-deductible and the account earnings are nontaxable until the participant begins withdrawing from the plan—no sooner than age 59½ and no later than age 70½— at which time all withdrawals are fully taxable as ordinary income. Like a life insurance policy, these plans permit the participant to name beneficiaries (an individual or a trust) who will receive the account balance if he should die before withdrawing it himself.

Unless the participant dies or becomes disabled, withdrawals made before age 59½ are penalized at the rate of 10% of the amount withdrawn and are fully taxable as income, but some financial advisors argue that, because the earnings on such deposits are compounded tax-free, paying a penalty for early withdrawal may still leave the participant with a higher yield than he would receive from a nonsheltered investment. Also, you can start annuity distribution from your IRA, prorated over your lifetime, at any time you wish, without paying the 10% penalty.

Either type of account can be opened with a bank, a mutual fund, or a stock broker, and the deposits can be used to purchase any of the investment instruments they offer. Stock brokers offer "self-directed" plans, which permit the participant to trade actively in securities at his own discretion, but any plan permits a participant to shift his account from one investment instrument or institution to another at any time, and there is no limit on the number of accounts he can open, provided that his total annual contributions do not exceed the permitted maximum.

Although an IRA or Keogh plan may be owned only by the participant and is normally not transferable, it combines some of the features of a revocable and an irrevocable trust, for which the bank or other financial institution functions as the participant's trustee and the participant, during his lifetime, functions as both grantor and beneficiary.

As in an irrevocable trust, the accumulation is not available to the participant's creditors (although it may be transferred by order of a court as part of a divorce settlement and for alimony payments and child support); its yield is not taxable to the participant (until withdrawal); the participant may not borrow from it or use it as collateral for a loan; and it is not considered part of the participant's taxable estate unless the estate itself has been named as the account beneficiary or unless it is withdrawn in a lump sum, either by a beneficiary or by the participant. It is not considered part of the taxable estate if the withdrawal is taken in the form of annuity or similar payments extending over 36 months or more.

As in a revocable trust, an IRA or Keogh plan participant does not lose ownership or control of the funds; he can use them at any time. Although he will pay a penalty if he withdraws before age 59½, he regains unrestricted use of them after that age.

As in the case of life insurance policies, it is important that beneficiaries and contingent beneficiaries be named on the plan's account. If one of the intended beneficiaries is a minor or an incompetent adult, the designated beneficiary should be the trustee of a living or testamentary trust set up for his benefit so as to avoid the need for (and limitations of) a guardianship or conservatorship. If the estate becomes the beneficiary through default—if, for example, no beneficiary survives—the entire account balance becomes subject to probate as well as to federal estate and state inheritance taxes.

CONDOMINIUMS AND COOPERATIVES
(SEE ALSO REAL ESTATE)

Problems involving condominiums and cooperatives usually relate not to the form of ownership (which can be any one of the forms described in Chapters 2 through 5) but to the rights conferred by ownership, since both these housing types differ from each other and from the conventional single-family house or rental apartment.

Condominiums

The buyer of a condominium unit buys two separate properties: (1) a housing unit, and (2) a share of the land on which it is built, including such amenities as lawns, walkways, tennis courts, laundry rooms, elevators, etc., whose use and maintenance of such "common areas" are shared by the other unit owners in the condominium. In some condominiums each unit owner buys an equal share of land and amenities; in others, the size of each owner's share is determined by the size of his unit. The buyer's ownership of the unit is documented by a regular deed, his share of the community property by a "declaration," or "master deed," and his obligations are set forth in the condominium bylaws.

The buyer can purchase both the unit and his share of the land and amenities with cash, or with a land contract, with a conventional mortgage, and no condominium owner is financially responsible if another owner defaults on his mortgage or land contract. Whatever his financing arrangements, however, he is obligated to pay a monthly association fee, determined by the board of directors of the owners' association, to cover insurance, services (e.g., snow and trash removal), and maintenance costs for the shared amenities.

The owner of a condominium unit has essentially the same control over his property as the owner of a conventional house. He can mortgage it, sell it to anyone he chooses, and use it for any purpose not prohibited by the bylaws and local zoning ordinances. And, of course, he is personally responsible for its maintenance. Control over and maintenance of the land and amenities, however, lies in the hands of the owners' association, and each owner's voice in the association's decisions is limited to the size of his share. Thus, if a majority of condominium association members votes to approve the construction of a swimming pool, each individual member will be assessed for his share of its construction and maintenance even though some may have voted against it.

Cooperatives

A cooperative differs from a condominium in several respects. The "buyer" of a unit (usually an apartment) in a cooperative does not actually purchase the unit; instead, he buys from the cooperative corporation shares of stock, the number of shares depending on the size of the unit. Each share is assessed a monthly charge to cover the building's taxes, mortgage payments, and maintenance costs. In addition, each shareholder signs a lease that specifies a fixed monthly rental for the unit he intends to occupy.

The fact that the buyer of a cooperative unit owns shares in the corporation and holds only a lease rather than legal title to a piece of real property has several consequences. First, financing may be more expensive and difficult to obtain, since it must be done through a personal loan, with the shares pledged as collateral, rather than through a conventional mortgage or land contract. (Some co-op boards require buyers to pay cash; others permit no more than 50% to 75% of the purchase price to be financed.) Second, if any one occupant defaults on his monthly assessments, the assessments of all the other co-op unit owners will probably increase, since the fixed costs of the building will have to be met regardless of the default. Lastly, the owner has even less control over his investment than the condominium owner. Not only may he be assessed for improvements that he opposes but, in some cooperatives, he may sell his shares only to the co-op corporation or to someone of whom the corporation approves.

CEMETERY LOTS

In some respects, cemetery lots are similar to other types of real estate. The lot can be owned in any of the forms described in Chapters 2 through 5. Ownership is evidenced by a deed and can be transferred by sale, gift, will, or trust. And, like other real estate, the lot is subject to eminent domain should the government decide to use the cemetery for a reservoir or some other public project for which it can prove "public necessity."

There are, however, some significant differences, most of them involving restrictions that do not apply to other real estate. To begin with, although a cemetery lot is not taxable, the cemetery may assess a compulsory maintenance fee or require an endowment to assure "perpetual care" of the lot and any graves it contains. In addition, although ownership includes an easement that permits the owner to use the cemetery roads and walkways to get access to the lot, such access is subject to the rules of the cemetery.

Use of the lot is, of course, restricted to burials, and the number of burials is limited to the number of grave sites contained in the lot, although some cemeteries permit the burial or two or more crematory urns in a single grave site. Certain specifications relating to the grave, such as the mandatory use of a vault or grave liner, may be imposed by the cemetery even though they are not mandated by state law. And, although the lot owner is permitted to install a grave marker, which remains his personal property, the size and style of the marker may be subject to cemetery regulations.

Because state law permits the sale of a cemetery only on the condition that it will continue to function as a cemetery, the rights of the lot owner are guaranteed should the ownership of the cemetery change hands. These rights may terminate, however, if the cemetery is abandoned by its owners.

Perhaps the most important restriction involves resale. Some cemeteries prohibit resale of a lot to anyone but themselves, thus exercising complete control over the resale price.

C H A P T E R 7

SITUATIONS THAT NEED SPECIAL CONSIDERATION

In explaining the various forms of ownership in Chapters 2 through 5, we were forced, for the sake of clarity, to make certain assumptions and to rely on a number of stereotypes. We assumed, for the most part, that our readers generally were comfortably situated in the middle-income range, had a level of indebtedness that was manageable, were (or would be or had been) married, were concerned with financing or subsidizing the education of their children, and intended, on their death, to leave their accumulated assets to their survivors.

In real life, of course, many people do not fit this stereotype. Some live together without marrying, and some of these have or adopt children. Of those who marry, large numbers do not stay married. Some people are continuously threatened by creditors; others face bankruptcy as a consequence of overspending, job loss, disability, or very high medical bills, which they are forced to pay because they have just enough assets to disqualify them from various government benefits.

This chapter, therefore, deals with situations that, although they are not part of the stereotyped—or at least the idealized—pattern of modern American life, are common enough to be encountered by a significant number of people.

Like the preceding chapter, this one need not be read systematically from beginning to end. Although we have attempted to rank the situations from most common to least common, the reader is best advised to browse through the headings and to read the text that follows only if it seems relevant or interesting.

DIVORCE

Aside from its emotional costs, a divorce has serious economic consequences in terms of alimony and child-support payments and, very often, a reduced standard of living for both partners. Our discussion here, however, will concentrate on only two of the economic issues: the division of property and the tax consequences.

Division of Property

In 42 states, the property of a marital couple is regarded as "separate." That is, upon divorce each spouse retains what he or she owned before the marriage plus any gifts, inheritances, and income from investments made as an individual. Even assets held in joint tenancy will be scrutinized as to the source of their acquisition rather than automatically divided equally. Strictly interpreted, the division of property on such a basis may well leave a non-wage-earning wife and mother with virtually nothing except whatever alimony and child-support payments are ordered by the court and ultimately collected.

Today, however, 15 of these 42 states do not adhere to this doctrine strictly. In these states marriage is regarded as a joint venture, and property is divided "equitably" so as to ensure the non-wage-earning spouse at least some measure of economic justice. Property held jointly is likely to be divided without regard as to which of the partners' earnings acquired it.

Eight states (Arizona, California, Idaho, Louisiana, New Mexico, Nevada, Texas, and Washington) are so-called "community property" states (see Chap. 8). They consider all assets acquired during the marriage to be the property of both partners, and in the event of a divorce the assets must be divided equally. Assets owned by each partner before the marriage or acquired by gift or inheritance during the marriage, however, remain separate and are retained by each spouse.

Such special "assets" as pension rights deserve careful consideration. A dependent wife, for example, might decide to postpone filing for divorce if she were aware that, upon her ex-husband's death, she would be entitled to Social Security survivor's benefits if the marriage had lasted at least 10 years.

Tax Consequences

Alimony payments, child-support payments, and deductions for dependent children are likely to affect the income tax liabilities of both partners. As we shall see shortly, a property settlement also may produce a capital gains tax liability for one of them. Hence, divorce negotiators need to bear in mind the tax consequences of each of their proposals, since often the same goal can be achieved in two ways, one of which offers significant tax advantages.

Alimony payments are tax-deductible by the partner who pays them and reportable as income by the partner who receives them provided that:

1. payments are required by an official agreement, whether a divorce separation, a court decree, or a written agreement between the parties;
2. the couple lives apart;
3. the payments are made in the form of cash, check, or money order and there is no liability to make payments after the death of the recipient;
4. the payments are for the general support of the recipient and not exclusively for child support or to settle loans or other obligations;
5. the payments for the first three years must not be excessively front-loaded. If annual payments do not decrease by more than $10,000 from either of the first two years to the next, this requirement is satisfied.

Child-support payments are neither deductible by the party paying them nor reportable as income by the child or by the child's custodial parent or guardian, regardless of which parent claims the child as a dependent on his or her tax return.

Since some parents about to enter into a divorce settlement agreement have the option of specifying payments in the form of either alimony or child support, their choice may well be governed by the tax consequences. If the paying parent is the only significant income earner, or is in a much higher tax bracket than the recipient, designating the payments as alimony might be preferable, especially since alimony is tax-deductible even if the payments take account of the needs of the children. In other circumstances, however, designating the same payments as child support rather than alimony may be preferable because it has no tax consequences for either parent.

Tax consequences, of course, are not the only consideration. Alimony payments usually terminate when the recipient ex-spouse remarries, although if the ex-spouse remains unmarried, they may be structured to decrease when each child reaches the age of majority. Child-support payments usually continue until each child reaches a specified age.

Tax exemptions for dependent children may involve more than the statutory $2,350 exemption; they can include the deduction of medical expenses incurred by the dependent child. A dependency exemption can be claimed by only one of the parents, usually the one who has custody of the children for the greater portion of the year. The parent who does not have custody may nevertheless claim the exemption provided that:

> for a decree signed before 1985, he or she provides at least $600 during the year for the support of each child and there is a court decree or a written agreement specifying that he or she is entitled to the dependency deduction,

or

> after January 1, 1985, he or she obtains from the custodial parent a written exemption release, using IRS Form 8332, and attaches it to his or her tax return.

Transfers of property resulting from a divorce settlement can also have serious tax consequences. A house or other property, such as securities, may be transferred from one spouse to another as part of a divorce settlement. At one time, the IRS treated such a sale as a transfer subject to capital gains tax, but today divorce-related property transfers no longer trigger a capital gains tax at the time of the transfer. However, the spouse who receives the property must treat it as acquired at the original purchase price. When the property is sold, the difference between the sale price and the original purchase price will be subject to capital gains tax.

Tax deductions on mortgage interest and real estate taxes depend on the terms of the divorce settlement and the terms of the mortgage. If the house remains in co-ownership (e.g., tenancy in common) between the divorced partners, mortgage payments cannot be deducted as alimony but the interest and real estate tax deductions may be claimed by the person(s) making the payments.

If both partners are liable for the mortgage and the divorce decree or separation agreement specifies that mortgage payments are to be made out of general alimony, half of the payment may be deductible (as part of the alimony) by the paying party and taxable as income to the recipient; the interest and real estate tax deductions are divided between them.

If alimony payments are being made under an informal agreement (under which alimony is not deductible), mortgage payments and real estate taxes should be paid directly by the partner in the higher tax bracket so that he or she can gain maximum advantage from these tax deductions.

Given the complexity of the issues, the wide variations in individual circumstances, and the numerous alternatives available, it is usually preferable for spouses who are planning a divorce to negotiate between themselves a detailed separation agreement concerning the division of property, alimony, child support, and responsibility for debts and present it to the judge presiding over the divorce proceedings. Unless the partners are implacably hostile to each other, they are likely to reach a compromise far more satisfactory to each of them than the agreement reached by competitively aggressive lawyers or the sometimes arbitrary division ordered by a busy and uninterested judge.

SINGLE PARENTHOOD

Although single parenthood, through adoption, death, divorce, or co-habitation, may occur at any stage of adult life, problems involving ownership are most likely to confront the single parent who has minor children and the elderly single parent with adult children.

The single parent of minor children may be inclined to protect their future by placing assets in joint ownership with them. This is usually inadvisable for several reasons. First, regardless of the nature of the assets, joint ownership involves some loss of control. And if the assets include real estate, the parent will not be able to sell the property unless a conservator is court-appointed for the minor, because minors are without legal capacity to convey title to real estate themselves. Even when a conservator has been appointed, he is not permitted to transfer the child's interest in the realty back to the parent. Moreover, as soon as the child reaches the age of majority, the conservator's authority terminates and whatever assets he has been safeguarding become immediately available to the child.

The options that the single parent has for avoiding these difficulties depend on the type and the value of the assets involved. If they consist of personal property and their value is low, the parent can retain them in his or her own name and will them to the child in the expectation that they will pass to the child through "small estate" proceedings (see Chap. 2) and thus avoid full probate. If the assets consist of bank deposits and their value exceeds the state's "small estate" maximum, a Totten trust (see Chap. 4) will give the parent full lifetime control of cash but pass it to the child automatically on the parent's death. A revocable living trust (see Chap. 4) provides the same advantages as a Totten trust but can include a wider variety of assets and—more important—can specify the schedule and conditions under which the child can have access to the assets, thus preventing the child from automatically gaining control of all the assets on reaching majority.

Elderly single parents of adult children are especially likely to be attracted to joint ownership of assets with their children in order to avoid probate. But such an arrangement lessens the parent's control over his assets and exposes a portion of them to the children's creditors. Moreover, if a home is placed in joint ownership with an adult child, the parent risks losing the homestead tax exemption—a reduction of property taxes that some states offer to elderly or disabled residents whose income does not exceed specified limits.

As in the case of the single parent with minor children, the elderly single parent should consider retaining assets in individual owner-ship and willing them to the children, forgoing avoidance of probate for the sake of greater control and safety. Alternatively, a Totten trust is useful if the assets consist of modest amounts of cash, or a revocable living trust if the assets are varied and the parent desires the many advantages of this useful estate-planning tool.

SECOND MARRIAGE

The kind of second marriage most likely to present ownership problems is that between two middle-age widowed or divorced persons either or both of whom already have children. In such situations each partner may be torn between a concern for the security of the other and a desire to leave at least some assets to his or her own children.

Joint ownership must be used with caution if at all in this situation, because on the death of one spouse, the survivor inherits all jointly held property with no legal obligation whatever to share any of it with the children of the deceased spouse. A will can, of course, provide for each spouse's children, but only to a limited extent, for a will cannot completely disinherit a spouse in the event that the marriage proves unhappy and short-lived. Worse yet, even if spouses agree to will their jointly owned property to the children of one of them after both die, if the parent dies first, the surviving nonparent is free to change his or her will so as to totally or partially disinherit the deceased spouse's children.

Two alternatives deserve consideration. First, a prenuptial agreement signed by both partners can specify precisely how the assets of each spouse are to be divided or disposed of in the event of separation, divorce, or death. Although such agreements are legally binding, most couples are reluctant to use them on the grounds that they introduce a grossly materialistic note into what is—at least at the time when they must be negotiated and signed—a highly romantic situation.

The second alternative, the revocable living trust, may provide a more satisfactory solution. If before the marriage each partner transfers all his or her property into a trust in his or her own name alone, each partner retains full control of his assets, the children of each are protected, and the other spouse can be left with nothing if the marriage terminates, whether by divorce or by death. There may be no need for either partner to disclose to the other the existence of the trust, although in the eyes of most couples such deception may be every bit as anti-romantic as the prenuptial agreement.

UNMARRIED COHABITATION

When a couple—heterosexual or homosexual—lives together without marriage, a state legally termed "unmarried cohabitation," the law distinguishes their relationship from marriage in ways that reflect society's traditional distaste for it despite its increasing prevalence. In general, both while their relationship persists and after it terminates, cohabitants have none of the protections the law provides for married couples.

Cohabitants, for example are not entitled to file a joint tax return, and neither of them may claim the other as a dependent and may not be able to buy an insurance policy on the other's life. Although one of them can acquire property from the other if they owned it in joint tenancy or in a living trust, the law does not entitle a surviving partner to any inheritance should the other die without leaving a will. And, of course, cohabitants cannot claim the unlimited marital deduction with respect to the federal gift and estate tax or the exemption usually granted to surviving spouses with respect to state death taxes.

The Social Security Administration will not provide unmarried cohabitants the same old-age pension that it provides a marital couple, nor is a surviving female cohabitant entitled to a widow's pension, death benefit, or any other benefits to which widows are entitled. In fact, even while living with her partner, a cohabitant mother of children is, in the eyes of the law, in much the same position as a single parent.

When the cohabitation terminates, each partner is fully entitled to the property that he or she owned before the relationship began, and gifts exchanged between cohabitants belong legally to the respective recipients. Problems often arise, however, in connection with jointly owned property and child support.

If the relationship has endured for several years, and especially if it has resulted in children, some courts recently have regarded cohabitation as based on an implied contract and have used contract law to compensate the woman for her services and to require the children's father to provide child support. But this principle is not yet embodied in any laws related specifically to cohabitation.

Because a couple's preference for cohabitation instead of marriage is so variously motivated, no advice about ownership is likely to be universally acceptable. All cohabitants would probably do well to prepare and sign a cohabitation agreement that specifies property division and financial support, and a will or a trust specifying inheritance rights in the event that the cohabitation is terminated by death or separation. But most precohabitating couples, like most premarital couples, are likely to shun such an agreement as too materialistic and unromantic, while others may reject it as excessively restrictive.

In the absence of a formal agreement, cohabiting partners should be aware of the options open to them. If they see their relationship as permanent, a house can be bought in joint ownership to ensure the survivor's inherting it; otherwise sole ownership or tenancy in common may be preferable. An apartment can be leased jointly or only by the partner who intends to retain occupancy and the responsibility for rent payments. Shared bank and brokerage accounts and property bought with shared funds also can be held in sole ownership, in joint tenancy, in tenancy in common, or in a revocable living trust. In addition, if each partner intends that the other should inherit, each should sign a will or use a revocable living trust, either of which can be altered unilaterally if the relationship changes or terminates.

Homosexual cohabitants are even less protected than heterosexuals because they cannot look forward to the various advantages and protections available to spouses. Hence, they are in even greater need of a contract specifying financial obligations and property division, and a will or a trust specifying inheritance. Such a contract should not, however, specify the exchange of sexual services because this may render the contract unenforceable on the grounds that it is contrary to sound public policy.

OWNERSHIP BY MINORS

Although there is no legal obstacle to a minor's acquiring or owning property, minors retain the right, until they attain majority, to rescind many contract transactions that would be binding on adults. Hence, since few people are likely to enter into an agreement with someone who is not legally bound by it, in the absence of a trust created for the child, a conservator or guardian (see Chap. 2) must be appointed by the local probate court if assets of any significant value are to be managed. Similarly, if a damage claim is pending on behalf of the child, the wrongdoer or his insurance carrier, in order to ensure that any settlement is final and binding, will insist that the settlement be made with and signed by the child's court-appointed guardian, and not by the child himself.

A conservatorship or a guardianship terminates automatically when the child marries or reaches the age of majority, whichever occurs earlier. At that point all guardianship assets are distributed to the child, regardless of his ability to manage, invest, and protect them.

Not all gifts or bequests to minors require the appointment of a conservator or a guardian. Gifts can be deposited (and subsequent gifts accumulated) in a custodial account (see Chap. 4), which, like a guardianship, gives the minor complete access to the assets when he reaches majority, or in a trust for minors (see Chap. 4), which can be structured to postpone distribution of the assets until an age beyond majority.

Many states permit inheritances intended for a minor to be entrusted to his parent or guardian if the inheritance does not exceed a specific maximum (usually $5,000), but if a larger inheritance is intended it can be willed to either a living or a testamentary trust, which names the child as a beneficiary. Under such an arrangement, the donor can specify both the age and the conditions under which the beneficiary is to receive the property.

Assets held for a minor in a guardianship account or a custodial account may not be used for the normal expenses that parents are expected to meet, and probate courts generally believe, especially when large sums are involved, that funds should be husbanded carefully until the child reaches the age of majority. The court can, however, be requested by the guardian to permit use of the assets for nonessential expenses—for cosmetic surgery, for example, or for summer camp or music lessons.

In general, a guardianship is more restrictive than a custodial account or a trust for minors because the guardian must get court permission for disbursements and must periodically file an accounting with the court, whereas neither a custodian nor a trustee is supervised by the court, and both can make disbursements and investment decisions at their discretion.

INCOMPETENCE

In the eyes of the law, an incompetent person is one who, by reason of illness or injury, has been adjudged by a court to be unable to manage his financial affairs. Any contract made by an adjudicated incompetent is unenforceable against him.

In such circumstances, the court appoints a guardian or conservator to manage the incompetent's assets, pay his bills and other expenses, and render to the court an annual accounting of these activities. If competence is regained, the guardianship or conservatorship is terminated by the probate court and the individual resumes possession and control of his assets.

In the case of a severely retarded child whose incompetence promises to be permanent, parents may serve as conservators or guardians as long as they wish, but eventually they may find it advisable to establish a living or testamentary trust to ensure the child's material welfare after their own deaths. In such circumstances the trustee—perhaps a trusted relative or a bank or trust company—may be given responsibility for handling the beneficiary's assets and expenses and for finding and monitoring an individual or an institution to assume custody and take care of his personal needs.

If an incompetent is hospitalized in a public institution, the state may require that any assets he or she owns be used to meet custodial expenses. If the incompetent owns nothing, the family may, in some circumstances, be held responsible. Most states require a husband, if he is able, to bear responsibility for his wife's maintenance expenses (although not all states require a wife to pay for an incompetent husband). All states require parents to meet the maintenance expenses of a minor child, and some require them to do the same for an adult child. No state currently requires children to pay the maintenance or health-care expenses of their parents.

GUARDIANSHIP

Guardians are usually appointed by a probate or similar court to take care of persons who are legally incapable of managing their own affairs: physically or mentally incompetent adults and, more commonly, minor children. Any interested party can petition the local probate court for appointment as guardian, but in making the appointment the court uses as its primary criterion the best interests of the ward.

There are two aspects to guardianship: guardianship of the person and guardianship of the property. When little property is involved, these functions are usually combined in one guardian. But if a ward's assets are substantial—that is, if they are worth more than $5,000 or if they include any real estate—the court may appoint two persons: a guardian to serve in loco parentis for the minor child (or to take custody and care of the personal needs of an incompetent adult) and another, called a conservator, to manage the ward's assets. Anyone bequeathing a large inheritance to a minor may nominate a conservator in his will—either an individual or a bank or trust company.

Although the guardian of the person has very wide discretion in dealing with the ward—as much discretion as a natural parent in the case of a minor child—the discretion of the conservator is much more limited. What he may or may not do with the ward's assets is either governed by state law or is subject to approval by the probate court, to which he must submit annual accountings.

Because the intent of this control by the court is the conservation of the ward's assets, the investments permitted are rather conservative. Funds may not, for example, be invested in speculative ventures but must usually be held in federally insured interest-bearing accounts. In no circumstances may they be used in ways that directly or indirectly benefit the conservator or anyone other than the ward. And, although many guardians have a discretionary power to buy, sell, or exchange personal property on behalf of the ward, real estate transactions may require the approval of the probate court. In sum, the conservator must manage the funds far more prudently than he might if they belonged to him. The courts generally permit the conservator to spend the yield on investments for the current needs of the ward, but they are extremely reluctant to permit expenditure of the principal.

A guardianship terminates when the ward becomes legally able to handle his own affairs—when, for example, an incompetent adult regains competence or when a minor child attains the age of majority or marries before attaining the age of majority. At that time, the conservator files a final accounting with the probate court and distributes all remaining conservatorship assets to his former ward.

If you plan to leave a substantial inheritance to a minor, there are several alternatives that may be preferable to nominating a conservator in your will. A custodial account for minors (see Chap. 4), although in some states it cannot include real estate, can accomplish almost all the purposes of a conservatorship without the supervision of the probate court. The custodian can be named by your will and need not be approved by the probate court, bonded, or compensated for his services. Like a conservatorship, a custodial account terminates when the minor attains majority. Two other alternatives—the revocable living trust and the testamentary trust (see Chap. 4)—offer greater control, for you can specify any schedule you choose for the payment of income or principal to the minor beneficiary, and you can postpone distribution of any inheritance well beyond the benefic-iary's age of majority.

ELIGIBILITY FOR CERTAIN GOVERNMENT BENEFITS

Because many people have a strong aversion to "welfare" and not much regard for most of its recipients, and because they assume that "our sort of people" are unlikely to ever "live off the government," the tend to learn little about programs designed to help people in need. In reality, however, inflation, family break-up, fluctuations of the economic cycle, job losses, and catastrophic illness have in recent years brought numbers of middle-class people close to poverty. And lengthening life expectancy, coupled with changes in the structure of the American family, has made ruinously expensive nursing homes and extended-care facilities the only alternative for many of the elderly. Hence an understanding of the relationship between prop-erty ownership and eligibility requirements for these programs may be useful, if not for ourselves then for our aging parents.

There are two extensive programs to help people with low incomes. The Social Security Administration's Supplemental Security Income program (known as SSI) is designed to supplement the incomes of needy individuals who are over the age of 65 or are blind or disabled. The Medicaid program is intended to cover, for needy people, the many medical costs not covered by Medicare and private insurance. Eligibility for the benefits of these programs depends, however, not only on the applicant's income and health status, but also on the value of the property he or his family owns.

Supplemental Security Income currently provides income up to $446 per month for a single person and $663 for a couple, and some states contribute to and thus increase these amounts. To be eligible, a single person must not own more than $2,000 in real and personal property; the limit for a married couple is $3,000. As the second column of Table 7 indicates, however, certain assets are either fully or partially exempt from inclusion in these limits.

In order to establish eligibility for SSI, the applicant must answer the question "Have you sold or given away any money or property during the past 24 months?" An affirmative answer may have the following consequences:

Table 7
ASSETS EXEMPTED BY SSI AND MEDICAID

Asset	SSI	Medicaid
Home and attached land	Fully exempt	Fully exempt
Personal effects	Fully exempt	Fully exempt
Automobile	One vehicle, fully exempt	One vehicle fully exempt
Life insurance	Up to $1,500 cash surrender value but no limit if over age 70 or terminally ill	Up to $1,000 cash surrender value
Other assets	Burial plot and up to $1,500 in burial funds for each of you and your spouse	Burial fund

If the purpose of the transaction was to convert nonexempt assets into exempt assets—if, for example, the applicant sold common stock and used the proceeds to pay off a mortgage on his home or to buy a house that he will occupy as a residence—eligibility will not be affected.

If the transaction was made at full market value—for example, if a boat worth $1,500 was sold for $1,500—eligibility will not be affected except insofar as the applicant's assets exceed the limit.

If, however, the transaction was made below market value—if an aging parent sold his $5,000 stamp collection to his son for only $2,000—the Social Security Administration will include the $3,000 difference in determining eligibility unless the father can prove that the transaction was not carried out for the express purpose of establishing his eligibility.

If the transaction did not place the assets beyond the reach of an applicant—if, for example, an elderly widow placed her money in a joint bank account with her daughter or in a revocable living trust—the Social Security Administration will include the transferred assets in determining eligibility.

Eligibility rules for Medicaid differ somewhat from those for SSI and, because the Medicaid program is administered by the states, eligibility requirements vary widely from one state to another. In general, however, to qualify for Medicaid, an elderly person must meet both asset and income limits. He or she must have less than $1,300 in monthly income or be deemed "medically needy" by the state. Personal property is limited to about $2,000 in cash or securities, although a home of unlimited value, a vehicle, and some miscellaneous items, such as a burial fund, are exempt. In addition, there are limits to the assets that applicants may own.

Unlike the SSI maximums, which are based only on assets belonging to the applicant, Medicaid maximums include the assets of the applicant's "family group" — that is, the parents of a minor, or the married couple of which an adult applicant is a member. The Medicaid maximums vary with the number of people constituting the family group, ranging from $2,000 to $3,000.

As the third column of Table 7 indicates, certain assets are exempt, but nonexempt assets will be counted only if they are *available*. An asset is not considered available if (1) no market exists for its sale or (2) it is owned jointly with someone outside the family group, its sale requires the co-owner's consent, and the co-owner withholds this consent.

As in the case of SSI, the Medicaid applicant is not permitted to divest himself intentionally of excess assets shortly before applying for benefits. In fact, anyone found to have divested himself of assets for the specific purpose of establishing eligibility for Medicaid may be denied Medicaid for a period of up to 60 months, depending on the value of the gifted assets. However, the burden of proof that the assets were transferred for the purpose of establishing Medicaid eligibility rests with the state. If, for example, a father makes a gift of $15,000 to a son to enable him to start a business and six months later finds himself in need of Medicaid, the father is not likely to be denied benefits.

Even if you manage to exempt your assets and succeed in qualifying for Medicaid-funded nursing-home care, you cannot be certain that your exempt assets will be available to your designated beneficiaries. In 1993 Congress required that all states adopt "estate recovery programs," which enable them to recoup Medicaid-paid expenses from your estate after your death. However, careful estate planning, including the use of an irrevocable "Medicaid trust," can effectively insulate family assets and protect them for your beneficiaries.

Medical and nursing-home costs continue to outpace the general inflation rate. In recognition of this reality, as our parents age it may be advisable to help them transfer ownership of their property or convert it into exempt property, so as to avert the possibility that they will be denied eligibility for any kind of government assistance simply because the value of their assets slightly exceeds the specified maximums.

OVERINDEBTEDNESS: GARNISHMENT, LEVY, ATTACHMENT

Garnishment, attachment, and *levy* are three actions that can be taken against your property by an unpaid creditor or by a claimant in a damage suit against you. Because these measures are harsh, they are rather strictly regulated by state and federal laws and can be authorized only by order of a court.

If you are seriously delinquent in paying your bills, your alimony, or your child support, or if you are in default on a personal loan or a promissory note, your creditor can, of course, sue you. If you do not pay the amount due him after he has won the suit and obtained a judgment against you, the court will issue him a writ authorizing him to *garnish* part of any income you are entitled to receive from a third party—usually your wages or salary but also other forms of income with the exception of a pension, alimony, and child-support payments.

On receipt of the writ, the source of your income—the garnishee—is required to withhold the garnished amount from each of your paychecks and remit it to the court for distribution to your judgment creditor. An employer is prohibited from discharging you simply because your pay has been garnished. If you are not regularly employed, your creditor can garnish any of your assets held by a third party—a bank account, for example.

To protect debtors against destitution, both federal and state law limit the amount of employment income that can be garnished weekly. Under federal law, a garnishment cannot exceed 25 percent of the debtor's weekly earnings or the amount by which his weekly *disposable* income exceeds thirty times the current minimum hourly wage, whichever amount is less. State laws may limit this amount further. Such protection, however, does not extend to garnishment for child support, alimony, bankruptcy, or delinquency on state or federal taxes.

In addition, the court can order a *levy* against any personal property held by you. In that event the sheriff can seize your boat, automobile, or other personal property and sell it at a public sale, the proceeds of which can be used to satisfy the debt. If you have no personal property, a sheriff can be authorized to levy against your real property—your home, for example, which also can be the subject of a forced sale.

Unlike a garnishment or a levy, which are authorized only after a court has entered a judgment against the debtor, an attachment is an interim measure sometimes available after filing suit but before the entry of a judgment. If you are being sued for certain kinds of money damages—such as for failure to fulfill the terms of a contract—and if there is reason to believe that you will conceal your assets, destroy them, remove them from the court's jurisdiction, or transfer them into a form of ownership that is beyond the reach of your creditors, the court may issue a *writ of attachment* for property of yours that is equal in value to the amount claimed in the lawsuit.

The attached property—a motor vehicle, for example, or a bank account—is placed under the control of the court, and you have no right to use or dispose of it until the suit against you is resolved. Attachment can be ruinous—if, for example, the entire inventory of a retailer is attached—but it is likely to be used only if the debtor has no other assets or shows signs of hiding or destroying them or disappearing from the state.

BANKRUPTCY

Given the pervasiveness of consumer credit, it is not surprising that increasing numbers of people find themselves overwhemed by a burden of debt that is compounded monthly by high interest rates and late-payment charges. Many of them reach a point at which full repayment is realistically impossible and the filing of a bankruptcy petition in the federal bankruptcy court seems the only solution.

Like divorce, bankruptcy carries far less stigma than it once did, and both the federal bankruptcy code and related state laws, which originally were drafted to deal with a failed business enterprise, have been revised toward greater leniency for the plight of the insolvent consumer. Because a bankruptcy adjudication must remain on the bankrupt's credit report for ten years, it can have a negative effect on the bankrupt's future attempts to get credit. However, many bankrupts report that they have little difficulty in obtaining credit, apparently because lenders believe either that bankruptcy has a salutary effect on the individual or that he is a safe risk because he will not be permitted a second bankruptcy for at least the next six years. According to one survey, only 35% of bankrupts reported difficulty in obtaining future credit.

Federal law recognizes several types of bankruptcy, including Chapter 7 ordinary bankruptcy for individuals, Chapter 11 bankruptcy for businesses, and Chapter 13 rehabilitation bankruptcy for individuals.

In a Chapter 13 bankruptcy, the court approves a renegotiation of the bankrupt's debts so that they are payable in full over a period of three years. Under this arrangement the bankrupt is relieved of financial pressure and all creditors receive what is owed them, although payment is delayed.

In a Chapter 7 bankruptcy, the court appoints a trustee to collect and liquidate the bankrupt's assets and distribute the proceeds pro rata among the creditors. Once this is done, the debts are fully discharged. The bankrupt gets a fresh start, but few creditors are paid in full, since liquidation of the bankrupt's assets is unlikely to satisfy 100 percent of his debts.

A Chapter 7 bankruptcy, however, is not the panacea that the foregoing paragraph may imply. To begin with, court fees and legal costs are likely to amount to at least $600 to $1,000, and many lawyers recommend against bankruptcy unless the debts it will discharge amount to more than $5,000.

More important, bankruptcy does not provide for the discharge of a *secured* debt such as a home mortgage loan or an automobile loan secured by a chattel mortgage. In such cases the bankruptcy trustee can sell the secured property and use the proceeds to satisfy the debt, although he cannot pursue the bankrupt for any deficiency between the sale price and the balance of the loan.

A number of other obligations and debts—certain taxes, alimony and child support, government loans to students, and money, goods, or services obtained by fraud or under false pretenses—are not dischargeable by bankruptcy and remain payable by the bankrupt. If a person intending to file for bankruptcy attempts, within the year preceding the filing of his petition, to protect assets by giving them to a relative, placing them in his wife's name, or concealing them, such actions can be set aside if the trustee discovers them.

Both federal and state laws, however, protect a bankrupt from total indigence by exempting certain assets from the bankruptcy proceedings. Federal law, for example, permits the bankrupt to retain a $7,500 interest in his home, a $1,200 interest in a motor vehicle, bank accounts up to $400, jewelry up to $500, life insurance policies with a cash surrender value of up to $4,000, and up to $4,000 of household furnishings, tools of his trade, and other assets.* With respect to these exemptions, state laws are generally more liberal than the federal law. For example, California exempts a homestead for up to $75,000. It is, moreover, perfectly legal for a person contemplating bankruptcy to convert nonexempt assets into these exempt forms before filing his petition of bankruptcy, although conversions made within 90 days of filing may be subject to challenge.

Strictly speaking, a bankruptcy petition can be filed without the help of a lawyer. But the basic question of whether bankruptcy is the best alternative, the wide variations in state laws, the problem of identifying available exemptions, the matter of optimal timing, and the question of whether a spouse should join in the filing usually make a bankruptcy lawyer's assistance worth its cost.

---

*Federal exemptions also include income from Social Security, disability benefits, unemployment compensation, pension, annuity and life insurance benefits, alimony, veterans' benefits, and welfare payments.

C H A P T E R   8

SPECIAL CONDITIONS IN COMMUNITY PROPERTY STATES

U nless you now live, have lived, or intend to live in
     Arizona, California, Idaho, Louisiana, Nevada,
New Mexico, Texas, or Washington, there is no need for you to read
this chapter. But current, former, and future residents of these
so-called "community property" states need to be aware that the
general forms of ownership described in Chapters 2 through 5 are to
some extent modified or restricted by the laws of these states.

   Although there are minor differences among their laws, the eight
community property states have a basic concept in common, and the
difference between them and the 42 so-called "common-law property" states is far more important than any differences among the eight.
This chapter will explain the concept of community property and
outline its implications for the various ways in which real and
personal property can be owned.

The Concept of Community Property

In the 42 common-law states, a single or married adult can hold
property in any of the forms described in Chapters 2 through 5 and
can exercise whatever ownership rights the particular form permits.
In these states a husband who is the couple's sole wage-earner can
choose to accumulate all his earnings in his own name, giving his wife

nothing more than an allowance for personal and household expenses. The wife would have no assets of her own and, should the husband desert her, she might well become destitute. In case of divorce, her settlement would depend heavily on the aggressiveness of her lawyer and the discretion of a judge.

In the community property states, by contrast, property acquired by either partner during a marriage, whether through earnings, acquisitions, or investments, automatically becomes *community* property; that is, each partner is immediately entitled to half of it. This ownership is not the same as joint tenancy, because it does not provide for automatic inheritance of the entire property by the survivor. Rather, it is essentially a tenancy in common, because each partner has full ownership and control over his half, not only during the marriage but also after the marriage has been terminated by death or divorce.

Traditionally, the husband has had the right to manage the community assets, but he must manage them with due regard for his wife's interests. In some states he may not transfer community real estate without her consent; in some he has no control over her earnings; and in most of them his management role is more like that of a trustee than of an outright owner, which, of course, he is not. However, several states have passed legislation entitling the wife to an equal role in managing community property.

There are some exceptions to the general rule defining community property. The exceptions, termed "separate" property so as to distinguish them from community property, are as follows:

Assets belonging to each partner *before the marriage* remain under individual ownership and, during the marriage, income derived from these assets and property acquired with them remain separate.

Property owned by the couple prior to their residence in a community property state retains its original form of ownership and is not regarded as community property.

During the marriage, property given to, inherited, or recovered as a personal injury claim by one or both of the spouses retains the form of ownership in which it is given, willed, or recovered and does not become community property, although in some states the income produced by such property is regarded as community property.

In addition, none of the eight community property states places any restrictions on gifts between spouses; thus either spouse can give the other, as separate property, his own half-interest in any community asset. Similarly, either community property or separate property can be transferred by gift into joint tenancy.

There are several ways by which the community property laws can be circumvented. With the exception of Arizona and Texas, all community property states permit a couple to sign a prenuptial agreement specifying that no community property will exist during their marriage—an exemption that may be especially significant for spouses entering a second marriage and having children from a first marriage. In several states couples may, either before or during their marriage, or both, sign agreements specifying whether property already acquired or to be acquired will be regarded as community property.

Notwithstanding these exceptions, the law of community property can be highly restrictive. If separate and community assets are comingled in the purchase of new property, that property is likely to be deemed community property. If community assets are used to acquire real property located in a common-law state, that property will be regarded as community property regardless of the laws of the state in which it is located. And if a couple moves from a community property state to a common-law state, any community property acquired in the community state will continue to be regarded as community property. On the other hand, property owned by a spouse or a couple who moves from a common-law state to a community property state will retain its original form of ownership after the move.

Protection of Spouses

The principal intent of community property laws is to recognize the economic contribution of the non-wage-earning spouse—usually the wife—and to offer her a measure of economic security. Indeed, it has been suggested that the community property states originally adopted the laws in an effort to attract female settlers during frontier times.

The laws also offer protection to spouses entering a second marriage. Because all assets that such spouses bring to the marriage are regarded as separate, they need not be inheritable by the second spouse but can be left instead to the children of the first marriage. On the other hand, given the considerable instability of contemporary marriages, this same feature may severely penalize a spouse who has had very high earnings during a marriage that turned out to be short-lived.

Problems of Probate

One major disadvantage of community property as a form of ownership is that it does not by itself avoid probate. When one spouse dies, his probate estate inevitably includes half of all the community property, which is subject not only to probate administration but also to the claims of his creditors. By contrast, property held in joint tenancy, tenancy by the entirety, or a living trust avoids probate administration and, in some states, is exempt from claims by the deceased owner's creditors. In addition, community property is more likely to be subject to state inheritance taxes than property that is jointly owned.

Accessibility to Creditors

The accessibility of community property to creditors varies from one state to another. In all states creditors can seize community property to satisfy debts incurred by the "community"—that is, the married couple. And with the exception of California, community property states assume that *all* debts incurred by either spouse were incurred for the benefit of the community. (California, in contrast, requires that the circumstances of each debt be examined to determine whether it is a community debt.)

Some states allow creditors to reach community property to satisfy the husband's individual debts whether they were incurred before or after the marriage, but most do not provide creditors the same access with respect to a wife's debts unless they were for "necessities" such as medical services, or were incurred when she was acting as her husband's agent—for example, using his credit card. In some community property states a wife's earnings, even though they are community property, can be used to satisfy her debts only. In all community property states a spouse's share of the community property is accessible to his or her creditors after death.

Gift and Estate Tax Consequences

Although the conversion of a spouse's earnings into community property may appear to be a gift to the other spouse, no gift tax is involved, because gifts between spouses enjoy an unlimited tax exemption. The same holds true when community property is converted to separate property.

With respect to federal estate tax, community property is treated similarly to property held in joint ownership—that is, one-half of it is included in the taxable estate of each spouse.

Whether or not the community property laws strike you as advantageous will depend on your personal and financial situation. It is important to recognize, however, that most community property states offer alternatives for residents whose circumstances make community property undesirable. Moreover, despite its apparent restrictions, the community property principle does not preclude your effective use of a number of the ownership alternatives described in Chapters 2 through 5. The rest of this chapter explains how these alternatives may be used to overcome any restrictions resulting from your former or current residence in a community property state.

SOLE OWNERSHIP

In community property states, as we have noted, separate property—that is, property owned by one of the spouses before the marriage and property acquired during the marriage by gift (including a gift from a spouse), by inheritance, or by the successful outcome of a personal injury suit—may remain in sole ownership. In addition, any income derived from separate property remains separate, as does any property acquired with separate assets.

Problems may arise, however, when the line of demarcation between separate and community property becomes blurred. If, for example, a spouse starts a business with separate capital, profits from the business *that are attributable to a return on that capital* remain separate, but profits attributable to his or her personal efforts become community property. Moreover, if he or she draws a salary from the business, it, like any other earnings, becomes a community property.

If both separate and community assets are used to begin or expand a business, meticulous records must be kept; otherwise all profits from the business will be deemed community assets. This is why the closely held corporation (see Chap. 5) may be especially useful for establishing and operating a business in a community property state.

Disputes over the ownership of separate assets may occur when they are created as the result of a gift between spouses. When a husband gives his wife a gift of part of his community property to hold as separate assets, his gift will be regarded as "completed"—that is, bona fide. When a wife gives property to her husband, however, and subsequently claims that a gift was not intended but that the transfer was made merely to facilitate his management of the assets, her attempt to recover her share is more likely to be successful. In such circumstances, a signed agreement clearly specifying the intentions of each spouse can avoid subsequent problems.

In community property states, the spouse's control over separate assets is much the same as in the common-law states, with one important exception. The owner of separate assets can bequeath them through his will in ways that disinherit his spouse and/or children, even in the absence of any other community property.

Creditors' access to separate property is identical in community property and common-law states. The husband's assets are not reachable by the wife's creditors and vice versa. The separate assets of both, however, are reachable to satisfy joint debts, joint bankruptcy, or joint damage claims.

If a couple separates without divorcing, the earnings and income of each of them after the separation are deemed to be separate property rather than community property. But in some states, if one of the spouses can persuade a court that the separation was caused by the other spouse's wrongdoing, the judge may deem the guilty spouse's income earned during the separation to be community property. Once a divorce takes place, however, separate property is not divided unless one party can prove that property that the other claims as separate is, in fact, community property.

In all other respects—accessibility to creditors, for example, or liability for income, gift, and estate taxes—separate property in community property states is no different from solely owned property in common-law states.

JOINT OWNERSHIP

As we have noted, ownership of community property, unlike joint ownership, does not provide for automatic inheritance by a surviving joint owner and, hence, the avoidance of probate. In all community property states, owners of *separate* property have the right to transfer it into joint ownership with a spouse, a third party such as a child, or both. The rules governing the transfer of *community* property into joint ownership, however, are varied and complex.

In general, community property states do not assume, as do common-law states, that the wording of the title to a piece of property reflects its true form of ownership. Thus, the fact that a stock certificate or a deed to real property purchased with community assets is inscribed with the names of husband and wife as joint tenants may not in itself prevent one spouse from subsequently proving to a court that it is actually community property. Similarly, on the death of one spouse the property purporting to be jointly owned may not automatically pass to the survivor; instead, for example, half of it may be claimed by the children of the deceased spouse's first marriage on the grounds that it was in fact community property despite its being titled as a joint ownership.

This situation might have been avoided had the spouses, before acquiring the property, managed to create separate assets (by agreement or by means of mutual gifts of community assets to each other) with which to buy the house. Alternatively, they might have specified in the deed or in a separate agreement that automatic inheritance was, in fact, intended. Lastly, each could have willed the property to the surviving spouse, but this would not, of course, avoid probate. In general, however, community property states take the position that property owned by spouses is presumed to be owned as community property and not in joint ownership.

These problems with respect to joint ownership apply only to those involving spouses. There is no restriction on the use of community assets for the creation of a joint tenancy with a third party. Thus, spouses can place their house or other separate property in joint ownership with an adult child so that the advantage of automatic inheritance becomes available.

The attractions of automatic inheritance (and the resulting avoidance of probate) do not, however, always outweigh the advantages of community property. Under community property law each spouse has immediate and unrestricted access to half of the community assets. This is an advantage not always available under joint ownership. For example, one co-owner cannot sell half of a house owned in joint ownership but is free to do so if the house is owned as community property. As we have noted, the community property principle also offers substantial protection to spouses entering a second marriage with considerable assets and with children from a first marriage. Because all the assets acquired before the marriage are

separate, they can be given or bequeathed by will to the children of
the first marriage—an outcome that cannot be guaranteed through
joint ownership with the new spouse. And if the second marriage
terminates, one second spouse has no claim whatever to the separate
property of the other, either before or after the other's death.

TRUSTS

All the principles governing trusts (see Chap. 4) apply equally in
community property and common-law states. The only significant
difference is that in community property states each spouse has full
and immediate access to half of the community assets, and hence
each can use his share of the assets (as well as any separate property)
to establish a trust without the consent of the other.

On the other hand, there is nothing to prevent spouses from
establishing by mutual agreement a trust funded by community
property. This tactic may be especially useful in community property
states because it not only avoids probate but may also result ultimately in the reduction or avoidance of federal estate tax upon the
death of the surviving spouse.

THE CLOSELY HELD CORPORATION

The laws governing incorporation may differ slightly among the
community property states as well as among the common-law states,
but the basic principles remain the same.

As in the case of trusts, a corporation can be capitalized by one
spouse using separate property and/or his or her half of the community property, but the corporate structure is an especially useful
device for segregating separate assets from community assets and
thus segregating the resulting dividends. If a certain number of
shares are purchased with separate property and other shares are
purchased with community property, the dividends paid on each lot
can be unmistakably classified as separate or community assets.
Salaries paid to spouses, however, will usually be classified as
community property.

INDEX

closely held corporations as
providers of 88, 99
ownership of 130–131
proceeds of 3, 24
revocable trusts 69
limited liability companies
(LLCs) 119–120
living trusts *see* revocable trusts
LLCs *see* limited liability
companies
loans, interest-free 76–79

M

marriages, second 146–147
in community property states
163, 167–168
Medicaid 153–155
meetings, of closely held
corporation 101, 115, 116
mineral rights 125–126
minors
custodial accounts for 5,
80–83, 150, 152
as joint tenants 34, 38
ownership by 149–150
trusts for 83–84
mortgages 129–130
motor vehicles
as corporate expenses 88
ownership of 25, 123–124
registration of 36
municipal bonds 4

N

naming of corporations 108

O

ownership
individual *see* sole ownership
joint *see* joint ownership
restraints on 1–3

rights of 2–4
sole *see* sole ownership

P

parenthood, single *see* single
parenthood
partnership agreements 51–52
partnerships 49–55
payable-on-death beneficiary
designation 32
personal holding companies 91
personal property 121–123
assignment of 37
and real estate 128
registration 122
in safe deposit boxes 135–136
personal representatives 15–16
pour-over will 69–70
power of attorney 9–13
probate
avoidance of 33–34
through incorporation 88
through joint tenancy 5, 33
through revocable trusts
63–64, 67
in community property states
164
and sole ownership 14–16
and unfunded trusts 70
professional corporations 93–95
property *see* community
property states; personal
property; real estate

R

real estate
condominiums *see*
condominiums
cooperatives *see* cooperatives
cost basis of 39
and divorce 144–145